HOPE OVER HYPE

Choosing Forever In A Right Now World

ROB CHIFOKOYO

HOPE OVER HYPE

Written by Rob Chifokoyo

Copyright © 2019 by Rob Chifokoyo

ISBN: 9781703759099

Edited by Ryan Peter, ryanpeterwrites.com

Graphics and inlay design by Dan Hagemann, hagemanncreative.com

Cover Photo: Katie Baab, kateleigh.com

www.robchifokoyo.com

info@robchifokoyo.com for queries

This is for

Jesus.
Lisa.
Hope.
Nakai.

CONTENTS

FOREWORD

Almost fifteen years ago I pastored a youth group at a mega church located in an upmarket neighbourhood in Harare, Zimbabwe. Every Friday night, teenage kids from mostly wealthy backgrounds showed up to enjoy the well-equipped band that led worship, or hang out with boyfriends and girlfriends. Somewhere in that whole mix of excited hormones and entitled attitudes they tried to find God. As a pastor I often wondered how many of these kids actually thought about or even believed any of what we did. I remember vividly, one Friday night after youth session was done and most kids had been picked up by their parents, a kid walked up to me and asked if I could give him a ride home since we lived in the same area. He was a cool kid and by "cool" I mean he was part of the in-crowd. He didn't overtly show that he was madly in love with God; he just kinda coasted. Later, he would confess he only came to youth group to "enjoy the Friday night vibe".

For many months he and I rode home and just talked. And that began a relationship with the unlikeliest future evangelist I would come to know.

Rob Chifokoyo was inquisitive. Not just about faith in God but about my personal faith, and that challenged me deeply. I came to know that Rob was a little different from the kids he desperately wanted to hang out with. Firstly, he didn't come from a wealthy family, and secondly, unlike most kids who definitely knew they'd go to university outside the country, he didn't know if he'd ever get that opportunity. What I didn't know was that Rob's experiences with God were much deeper than I had observed at youth group.

Years after I had moved on from that church, Rob started a non-denominational youth outreach program in Harare. He called it "Dare to Serve". With a few friends, and not a dime to his name, Rob began ministering to all sorts of neglected communities. They reached out to street children and even started a street school for them. He mobilised volunteers during school holidays to help a struggling pastor build his church. One time he called me, asking if it was a good idea to go into the red light district and minister to prostitutes on Valentines Day by giving them roses and telling them that God loves them. I was scared and thought they'd get arrested but that was the depth of Rob's desire to deliver hope to people. You'll have to ask him if they went through with it. I'll never forget the time Rob and his friends (again without a cent in their pockets) organised the hugely successful 99-4-1 youth conference in Harare. They named it after the story in the Bible in which Jesus teaches about the shepherd who leaves his ninety-nine sheep to go and look for the one that was lost. I couldn't believe this was the same young man who was just another kid at the youth group. Perhaps the time when I knew God had some amazing plans for his life was when I heard Rob had fallen sick with kidney failure. I remember seeing him lying emaciated in a hospital bed and wondering if this was the end. We prayed asking for breakthrough and what followed was a miracle that few could imagine.

In recent years, the Lord has put me on a challenging mission. He has caused me to challenge the wickedness and brutality of our government in Zimbabwe. This has meant that I have spent many months in prisons and courts facing multiple treason trials and painfully being separated from my family for years. I'd never have guessed that the kid from the youth group who asked me for a ride would one day be a source of strength and hope during this time. Without fail he has reached out constantly, mobilising prayer and support for me. If you had asked me years earlier to pick a kid from the youth group who would one day rally hundreds of people to serve their community with acts of love, who would believe God for the youth of a city to be saved, and who would trust that God would save his life miraculously as he lay dying in a hospital bed—and who would strengthen me in my time of tribulation—I'd never have picked Rob Chifokoyo. But God did and gave him a unique grace to inspire hope and breakthrough. I'm so blessed by the exploits that God has caused Rob to do and as he continues this journey of changing the world with the love of God. I pray much more encouragement and wisdom would come from him as he teaches and pursues the heart of God for this generation. Turns out this kid who asked me for a ride on a Friday night after youth group is a world changer.

• Evan Mawarire

INTRODUCTION

What's up people?

Quick question. What do chicken sandwiches, fidget spinners, Chewbacca Mom, Alex from Target, Damn Daniel and Flappy Bird have in common?

The answer is, at one point or another they were the talk of the internet.

But where are they now?

Aren't you the slightest bit curious as to what happens after people go viral? They reach monumental heights almost completely by accident and then, poof! The hype is gone and so are they. I'd like to think there is a mass grave somewhere in the middle of Nebraska where all the fidget spinners went to be with the Lord. I'd like to think that Chewbacca Mom went back to just being a Texan mom who finds the small things in life amusing; that Alex from

Target upgraded his prom date options; and that Damn Daniel got a lifetime supply of Vans, so he's good!

The point is the hype came. And it was real. Then the hype went. As *hype always does*. We should never forget that.

So, welcome to a book that I've been so hyped to write and my wife so hyped to read! Oh, and my mom and mother-in-law. They like reading my stuff. As for everyone else who reads this, I have no idea who you are and what you will think of the words I have miraculously placed in here. I say "miraculously" not because I'm using it is a figure of speech but because it actually *is* a miracle that I've been able to write this. See, every time I do something that normally requires a level of writing ability to accomplish, it's a miracle. Maybe you're like me, always told you can't do this because, well, you fill in the blank. But you keep saying, stuff it, I'm gonna do it anyway, and it's gonna be awesome. That's me! Zero hype, zero expectations. I'm just a guy who didn't do too great in English class, willing to be used by a God who invented language (#towerofbabel). This opening part is just for you. I got a 'C' in English and this will be my second book. I've already superseded all my educational projections and I want you to know... so can you.

Now I'm a pastor and I can be a little long winded at times, but I thought that bit was important especially for readers like myself. You have it in you. I want to encourage you to keep reading with that in mind.

So, where was I? Oh yes, you're hyped to read this

book. But what is this book about? Well this book is about seeing one great hope through a bunch of hype the world throws at us. This book is about rediscovering the truth in a world that is constantly selling us lies.

So what is the hope I'm talking about all through this book? It's that a God who created everything is ultimately the only one who knows how *everything* is meant to function. He has actually created stuff for our enjoyment, but there is a catch. The things He created are best enjoyed in the *way that He says they should be enjoyed*.

The good news is there are a million ways to reveal that hope, and there are sixty-six sacred books written just to reveal all this to us. We will always know where to go when we need to be reminded that God knows best and has always had our best in mind.

Now, if you're still tracking with me, I'm pumped 'cause you haven't put this book down yet. In fact, unless you know me personally or you're Zimbabwean, I'm pumped you opened this darn book despite not knowing how to pronounce my last name. Thank you for sticking with me.

So here is the deal. The hype is real. I mean everything is selling the hype and trying to make us ignore the hope. But my heart is incredibly expectant that if you were aware of the hope, you would be left with no choice but to desperately want to seek out God's best in everything.

It's incredibly difficult to think of God's plan for things like sex, relationships, money, body image as something better than the hype the world and media throw at us every single day. I will be the first to acknowledge that it may take more than just a book to realign our thinking. Being transformed into people that can live grounded in the never-changing hope of God, rather than the ever-changing message of the world, is not an easy task. The Holy Spirit is going to have to do a mighty work in all of us, myself included, for our hearts to be shifted.

I am a storyteller by nature because that is what Africans are good at. So then let me tell you a story.

I want you to think of a time when someone broke a promise you hoped with everything they would keep. I want you to go back and think for a second how that felt. How it felt to have hope snatched right out of your hand like that. See, I don't have to think too hard to get myself back to that moment. I remember when I was growing up in Zimbabwe there was a promise my dad would make often but would also constantly break. My father was my hero, like for any little seven-year-old. But my dad was no ordinary hero, he was a known public figure. I would hear his name in songs on the radio, policemen would recognize his name at police checkpoints and let us proceed with ease. It would just make me so proud. I would think, "That's *my* dad." My dad was a public figure because he managed one of Zimbabwe's biggest soccer teams for almost two decades. For the first fourteen years of my life, this is what my dad did on his weekends. I want you to think of the general manager of the second biggest sports franchise in your state, or even your country, and then think how popular or unpopular that guy is. Well, my dad was the Zimbabwean version of that guy you've just thought of.

So back to the promise. My dad would make this promise to my brother and I constantly. He would leave early in the morning on game day and tell us to be bathed and changed by a certain time. He would then promise that he'll take us to sit on the sidelines during the game, right next to the amazing soccer superstars we had on our calendars and who we would talk to our friends about. We may even get to hang out with the players at the sports club afterwards if we were lucky!

Can you imagine the weight of that promise to kids who idolize these athletes? We could hardly sleep when he would tell this to us. I mean, we would get to hang out with the likes of Joel Shambo, Shacky Tauro, Brena Msiska, Carlos Max... All these names are big legendary names in Zimbabwean soccer history. Just google them. Time and time again we would get ready and bathed. Then the time would come and kick-off would be fast approaching and our eyes would be fixed on the gate. It was almost time! A dream come true!

Five minutes pass. He's probably just late, he'll be here soon. Ten minutes. Maybe there was a delay on the field? Thirty minutes... one hour... and hope would start to disappear. We would think maybe he'll quickly drive here at half time or maybe he'll just take us to hang out at the club house after the game. Then the dreaded truth would unhealthily settle in our hearts like a quesarito settles in your stomach— he's not coming.

Hope was deferred and it was a feeling, even in our early years, which we didn't quite know how to process in our hearts.

Now the story doesn't end there. See, my dad didn't always leave us hanging. There would be one out of every twenty or so promises where he would actually come and take us to a game, and it would always be the greatest time ever. We would drive up to the V.I.P. parking, the security guards would open a special entrance for us, and we'd head through the locker rooms right to the sidelines. Or there would be times during a major cup final where he would take us to the National Sports Stadium and we would sit with these important dignitaries watching our team lift the Cup! It would be the most epic of times. "Unforgettable" is the word I would use to describe the feeling.

But, you see, the unfulfilled hope was always made much worse because there were times when it *was* fulfilled. The inconsistency was the thing that made those moments harder.

My mom, on the other hand, never broke a promise. If she said, "Be ready and bathed, I'm coming to get you," she came through. Now my mom's promises were smaller in comparison. She couldn't give us sideline access to the stars. She couldn't give us a seat in the V.I.P. section of the National Sports Stadium. Her promises were more like ice-cream treats, a drive around the neighborhood, or a train ride to visit cousins in Bulawayo. Even though those things were smaller, they were never ever broken promises.

See, hype delivers sometimes and it makes us feel a

certain way. I love my dad for trying to give us all these big moments and I'm thankful for what they were, but I do remember when the hype failed to deliver. Hope on the other hand is like my mom's promises. Not flashy but always consistent. I remember on one occasion when my mom returned from a trip to the U.S. She told us she would bring us each something. Our hope was rooted in the fact that she always delivers. When she opened her suitcases after arriving and started pulling out Jordans, Nikes and tons of clothes, we were blown away! She had gone over and beyond our expectations! We knew she always came through but we never expected she would exceed our expectations by that much! Sometimes hope gives you more than you hoped for when it is delivered.

As we journey through this book, I want you to know that hype is what it is... hype. It comes and goes and often-times leaves us bathed and ready to go with no one coming to get us. If hope deferred makes the heart sick then hype deferred pummels our hearts with a sledgehammer. We have a God who promises us some pretty huge things that fill us up with hope, while we have a world that sells us a whole lot a hype. God comes through consistently and His hope will never be put to shame. It may not be flashy in the eyes of popular culture but when that suitcase opens, we will find that His hope delivers above and beyond!

Hope you enjoy journeying with me through this.

• Rob Chifokoyo

AMBITION

I remember walking into the house after a long day at work and being greeted by an extremely excited wife.

"Rob, you have got to see this!" she said, panting she was so amped! "I've got to show you this thing I saw today!"

Lisa unlocked her phone and went to an Insta story from a lady she follows. All I could see were little hearts popping up on this woman's live feed in a way I hadn't quite seen before. It seemed like hundreds, maybe even thousands of women were following her... but why? What was she saying? What was she even doing? I couldn't quite exactly figure out what my wife was showing me. Was she a Kardashian? I mean those are the only people I knew who had that many likes for seemingly doing nothing!

After a little while I realized she was selling some type of lipstick and the big deal was that it didn't come off. She was inviting other ladies to get in on this new color they were soon going to release and that she had first dibs on. I tried to hide my skepticism as best I could. "Read the moment Rob," I told myself. "This is not the time to bring up the multi-level marketing documentary you watched a few months ago." This also wasn't the time to mock the product and ask how, if it doesn't come off, what you do when you eventually *want* it off?

Because I could see on my wife's face that she had found it. She had found that thing that almost everyone is looking for nowadays — a worthy side hustle.

We can't deny that we live in one of the most ambitiously driven times in history. This is the age of the social media gold rush where you can apparently control your own destiny if you get the right steps down. The woman my wife was showing me was making six figures from the comfort of her home by just selling lipstick on Instagram. Eventually I had to show Lisa the intro of *The Office* chapter 2 verse 19 - I mean season 2 episode 19, "The Pyramid Scheme." I may even followed her around saying, "When the son of the deposed king of Nigeria emails you directly asking for help, you help! His father ran the freaking country, ok?" Lisa was not amused!

Six figures though. It's worth a shot, right? All they need is $50 and for you to buy some stock and sell it, and you're off to the races. But the carrot that was dangling in front of my wife was this: you get to make an impact. You get to be somebody, influence many women around you, and enjoy life while you do it. If you're ambitious and you really work hard, you will be just like that woman in

Proverbs 31 who side hustles before the sun comes up and makes her family prosperous.

There is nothing in this world that will tell us what Jesus tells us about ambition. Jesus was anti worldly ambition and all about Kingdom ambition. He encourages us to be great by doing the *opposite* of what this world and all the Instagram 'influencers' encourage us to do. He tells us to be humble and to be the ones who are willing to serve rather than be served. Show me an Instagram influencer saying that, and meaning it? But at the center of all this hype around being ambitious is *us*! Let's be real here, people. We are doing all these things as a big "please notice me" as though our value is tied up in how much money we make or how many people think we are worth a repost or a tag. Yet Jesus looks at who is *last*. The servant is who God is shining upon, whether or not you feel it. He's looking in *that* direction!

> 5 "Everything they do is done for people to see: They make their phylacteries wide and the tassels on their garments long; 6 they love the place of honor at banquets and the most important seats in the synagogues; 7 they love to be greeted with respect in the marketplaces and to be called 'Rabbi' by others.

> 8 "But you are not to be called 'Rabbi,' for you have one Teacher, and you are all brothers. 9 And do not call anyone on earth 'father,' for you have one Father, and he is in heaven. 10 Nor are you to be called instructors, for

you have one Instructor, the Messiah. 11 The greatest among you will be your servant. 12 For those who exalt themselves will be humbled, and those who humble themselves will be exalted." (Matthew 23:5-12)

Jesus is talking about the big dogs of the day, the ones who are pretty much seen by all the people, and He is throwing out a challenge to His disciples. Jesus himself tells His followers to not allow worldly ambition be the goal of their spirituality. He shows them that the goal is to glorify Jesus and not themselves. Sometimes you have to be willing to be invisible! Replace 'Rabbi' with whatever title that you are seeking for right now. Replace the wide phylacteries with our social media pages and the places of honor and important seats with what we chase after and post about. Then ask: are you exalting yourself all in the name of hustling or "doing you"?

It's not about me, but it kinda is.

I remember going out to dinner with some friends after a church service one Saturday. We were out to get Mexican food, because you know, as an African living in America, Mexican food is the closest thing to a healthy African meal. So as we are eating our burritos, a group of young ladies walks into the restaurant. Almost immediately one of the girls pulls out her phone and starts taking pictures of me. Now at first, I was a little taken aback. Is she really taking photos of me? Like for real? The camera is pointed right at me. I'm getting convinced that she's gobsmacked by my amazing good looks. The longer this went on, the more my objection faded away and I started to think, "Wow. I really must be looking good. It has to be that zero fade my boy gave me at the barber shop the other day." I go from being offended to adjusting my position so I could give her my best side. My mind is racing at the thought of how I would later tell this story to my wife and remind her to stop taking this fine specimen of a man for granted and start appreciating this fine chocolate brotha'. I had the whole "I told you I'm premium chocolate" speech planned —all this time I thought I was Hershey's when I was actually Godiva!

What seemed like minutes went on and then the photoshoot took a sudden turn... she noticed me posing. I'm thinking I'm going to have to tell this girl that as flattering as it is to get my photo taken by random people, I've reached my limit. But she looks at me and suggests with her hands that I should look behind me. As I look I see her friend who seems to be working her first-ever shift at this restaurant and that's who she was taking pictures of! I went from thinking I was Idris Elba to Flava Flav in two seconds. Argh! I felt so puny and like the biggest idiot to just assume that this thing was about me. I mean how come it wasn't? Just look at my back page cover photo!

The reason I tell that story time and time again is because we live in a world that preaches that everything is about us, and I fell victim to that trap in the restaurant that night. Social media is always asking me how I'm doing or what's going on. Instagram has little hearts to remind me how much I'm loved when I share a picture; and almost every single commercial is telling me that I deserve better because I am *me*. How can we not think the world revolves around us when that much attention is being paid to us? However, the truth is this: the world doesn't revolve around you.

But if it doesn't revolve around you, then who does it revolve around? That is the question this book seeks to answer.

The heading of this chapter is about as honest as I can be about my life: "This may not be about Jesus." It may even be an accurate view of where the Church is. I'm a Christian, but there may be more truth in me saying that part of my desire to write this book is found in my own pursuit to be significant than in my pursuit to magnify Christ. I have to really search my heart to see if my motive is to reach people who need to know of God's love and the liberation the truth of the cross brings. That's right, I said it! We have to start where we're brutally honest about where we feel insignificant in order to be made whole.

Do we sometimes do things, even good things, in pursuit of something that would bring us a sort of self-centered fulfillment or contentment? Are our church programs, our vision, our podcasts really a means to broadcast a message that brings freedom? Or is it more about us building our brand in the name of Jesus? These are important things to ask and wrestle through in our pursuit of *godly* ambition.

CONTENTMENT

A big reason why we exist in this realm of self may lie in the truth of our discontentment. I mean, who wants to settle, right? Don't get me wrong, contentment is not to be mixed up with mediocrity. But we often use giving our best to God as our green light to keep chasing personal self-centered agendas that really have nothing to do with Him. We then end up on this constant treadmill of chasing after a fulfillment that we will never truly find.

Contentment is something Paul highlighted when writing his famous "thank you" note to a church in Philippi, and there is nothing about Paul that was mediocre. Paul was a beast when it came to crushing his goals. He freakin' wrote three quarters of the New Testament!

> 10 I rejoiced greatly in the Lord that at last you renewed your concern for me. Indeed, you were concerned, but you had no opportunity to show it. 11 I am not saying this because I am in need, for I have learned to be content whatever the circumstances. 12 I know what it is to be in need, and I know what it is to have plenty. I have learned the secret of being content in any and every situation, whether well fed or hungry, whether living in plenty or in want. 13 I can do all this through him who gives me strength. (Philippians 4:10-13)

Paul is writing these words from prison and thanking this church for their partnership with him in the work that

God set out for him to do. Did I just skim over the fact that a prisoner is talking to free people about being content? Can you imagine how much weight this carried? I've found myself in situations where I am complaining about how something is going wrong in my life and then I have a conversation with someone who is going through something worse, and yet they are not moping around and complaining. That gives me a fresh perspective on my situation. I can often walk around my local grocery store and complain about how they only have two types of almond milk, and then I talk to my friends in Zimbabwe and hear that they have no milk of any kind at all. That gives me real perspective.

I believe a way we can be less about ourselves and more about something that is greater than us is to gain a new perspective. Even though Paul is in prison, chained and denied freedom for the sake of the gospel, he is probably more free than the people he's writing to. He is not bound by discontentment and he graciously shares his secret to being content:

> "I have learned the secret of being content in any and every situation, whether well fed or hungry, whether living in plenty or in want." (Philippians 4:12)

Paul lets this church know that this thing called contentment didn't come naturally to him and that he had to learn it. This says something about human nature all around the world. We all have to learn to be happy with what we have but we most certainly don't have to teach ourselves to want more. See, if we do not truly find contentment in what we already have, we will constantly be looking for the next promotion, relationship, side hustle, financial milestone, or just a plain old new kitchen aid mixer. But if you're old enough to read then you're old enough to know that contentment is really a lot easier said than done. Contentment is not on the other side of anything. Contentment has to be learned where you are.

So what is this secret Paul has found and where is it? Or more like, who is it?

Paul describes in Philippians 4:13 that it is in Christ that he has found this secret of contentment. One of the most famously misunderstood verses in the Bible is what he says in that verse: "I can do all things through Christ who strengthens me." It is often taken out of context and made to mean only half of what it means. I say half because we normally see this verse when our favorite sports person is being interviewed before the big game and we translate it to mean we will win because we can do everything through Christ. We only associate this verse with a physical victory here on earth when it is probably more accurately quoted not when the quarterback is holding the Vince Lombardi or the Champions League trophy but rather when he is in the post-game interview after blowing a thirty point second half-lead in the biggest game of their lives.

See, Paul is saying it doesn't matter whether you have or don't have, whether you have victory or defeat. You can remain content because you have Jesus and He gives you strength to face victory with grace, and defeat with honor. Paul said he had to learn this in need and in plenty. Essentially he says Jesus has got to be the ground you stand on otherwise you will sink, whether you have much or are in need.

FOUNDATION

Now, full disclosure. I am no building expert. In fact the most I've ever done when it comes to building is helping my daughter construct her building block set. I'm terrible at doing anything D.I.Y. but with that said, even I know how important foundations are. The more we have a firm foundation the sturdier everything we build upon it will be. So we know that when you are building a house and the foundation is not quite right, things may look okay for a while but after a few years you will run into problems when external elements start to take their toll on the building.

So if we know the importance of this on a physical structure, what part do we believe solid foundations play in our spiritual lives, especially in our ambitious pursuits? How can we build our lives on a solid foundation so that when external elements shake us we are able to withstand them? The Bible tells us something that can help us understand what God says our solid foundation should be.

24 "Everyone then who hears these words of mine and does them will be like a wise man who built his house on

the rock. 25 And the rain fell, and the floods came, and the winds blew and beat on that house, but it did not fall, because it had been founded on the rock. 26 And everyone who hears these words of mine and does not do them will be like a foolish man who built his house on the sand. 27 And the rain fell, and the floods came, and the winds blew and beat against that house, and it fell, and great was the fall of it." (Matthew 7:24-27)

Here, Jesus is giving us the news we are all desperately in need of hearing when it comes to the question of significance. He says if He is your foundation, you're good to go, and any other foundation is sinking sand.

When it comes to our quest for significance and importance we ought to know that in Christ we are already completely and wholly loved. All the affirmation you have ever needed is displayed to you on a cross, with a spotless savior, taking on all our mess-ups, hang-ups and brutally taking a punishment we deserved in order to shout out a truth that reverberates throughout all of eternity—you are loved! Jesus is saying you don't have to worry about acceptance from anyone when you know that you are accepted by Him. What a beautiful truth and what amazing news! That is the thing that Paul has learnt that has led him to say, "I can do all things through Christ who strengthens me." He has found a foundation that is enough for him no matter the circumstance.

Without this firm foundation we start to desperately seek our significance in the approval and acceptance of others, a trap that's incredibly hard to get free from. If our foundation is not Christ we will never truly be content. Discontentment is a dumpster fire. It steals many things from you and also will never allow you to be happy for someone else's success because it makes you feel inadequate. Discontentment will never allow you to truly be generous because how can you give when you still don't have enough? Discontentment should never ever be allowed to drive the car that is your life.

As I look at the many ways discontentment can infiltrate our generation I wholeheartedly empathize. When I was in school, civvies day (the day when you didn't have to wear school uniform) was your opportunity to flex. This was your chance to show all your friends your coolest gear. Growing up, this was also a day that caused so much discontentment because all you could see was what you didn't have. Today, civvies day, is every day you turn on your phone and go on Instagram or Snapchat. Discontentment says you don't have enough. You don't have enough money, notoriety, material possessions and success. Really, that's what drives ambition right? Get bigger, get more! Enough is never enough!

I have a four-year-old daughter whom I love so much. She has the sweetest little heart and for a four-year-old she is incredibly aware of the needs of people around her! I am such a proud dad but when I see her being kind to others it takes it to another level. With that said, she is four, and four will do what four does. In the world of four-year-olds she's Mother Theresa but she's still stingy at times and illogically so. I remember once a family invited us over to their house out in Florida. I mean they blessed us with the airfare, lodging, the whole shabang and they even went a step further and offered to watch our kids while my wife and I went on a date. If you're thinking about where one finds friends like that then you get how grateful our hearts were.

While they were babysitting they decided to bake a batch of cupcakes with my daughter. Stick with me here, there is a reason I am telling you all this. I mean they did all of that for us but as the moment was fast approaching for the night to end I couldn't have braced for what would happen next. There must have been about ten cupcakes baked on a plate and big ones too, and the kind lady who had done all this for us asked my daughter for one. Just one out of ten. One. My daughter's answer to this one itty bitty request was a resounding Gollum sounding "No!"

Now if you're a parent out there and you're thinking, on a scale of one to Fergie's national anthem performance, how super embarrassing was that? Well, it's up there with Fergie! We tried to be as polite as we could and my wife may have even done that speaking-through-her-smile-threatening thing that moms do so well (if you know, you know!); or maybe she just gave our daughter the girl-if-you-know-what's-good-for-you look.But whatever we tried it seemed to make the situation even more embarrassing!

I feel like in many ways we are like four-year-olds when it comes to our hoarding nature, because our natural inclination is to want everything we see. It's why advertising is such a vital industry for brands. If they see it and we tell them they need it, they will come. We also want everything for the what-if moments. What if I need this someday? What if I suddenly don't have enough when I need it most? My daughter may have even been thinking, "What if I need more cupcakes tomorrow night? Or what if I drop one (or in this case, seven)?" This is us when we are not content. Discontentment says there isn't enough to go around, so you better hold onto all you can. We don't just reserve this for hogging material things alone but we also do this with things like praise for one another and support. You can like your friend's status and not lose something. You can praise work that someone else is doing or, dare I say, even share it for others to see without losing an iota of social media cred. Men don't say this nearly enough to one another and pastors in the same area definitely don't say this enough, for sure. There is room for you to like another status from a church down the street. There is room to encourage one another publicly so that the people you shepherd see the heart of Christ beyond the lies of the enemy. We don't have to constantly compare. This comparison stuff gives birth to, and breeds, discontentment.

COMPARISON

You know that moment when you finally get your acceptance letter from the one college you wanted to go to and, as you're about to post that picture with your letter to your social media, you see a little "1" on your notifications?

"Stacy hasn't posted in a while..." it says, and as you click, there it is. A picture of Stacy holding *two* acceptance letters with the caption below saying, "Hard choice to make ahead! Princeton or Harvard? Help me please!!!"

You look at your laptop and then down at your little-known farming town college that only but a few moments ago was more than enough for you but now seems so pathetic. You feel a sudden surge of discontentment. You were content before you saw Stacy's post but now the monster known as comparison has come in to sap any joy you had your hands on.

Maybe for you it's not about a university but it's your new granite countertops while your neighbor just got marble. Or maybe it's even your baby. Your friend's baby looks like a real human being and yours looks like Groot from Guardians of the Galaxy (which is really what babies are supposed to look like, right?). Now you're a little fearful of posting pictures of your own real-life baby! Or maybe you want to be an influencer just like Jenna Kutcher. You think to yourself, "I look like Jenna; I sound like Jenna; I'm a photographer just like Jenna," but when she posts pictures eating grapes off of her husband's nine pack it hits you—you look nothing like the Kutchers. Your husband does not look like that dude at all. You love your precious balding, microbrewery pooch husband but looks are not something Jesus assigned in his direction. He is not aging like a fine wine but more like a grape left in the sun too long, and he looks nothing like Mr Kutcher but more like a thinner version of Thanos.

Whatever the scenario, I know at some level you resonate with me here. Comparison is the thief that comes in the night to take away the joy of contentment and we now live in comparison-ville. Everything around us is showing us the life we don't have and if you're like me you are so tempted to post about your highest highs so that you can add to the false narrative of living a life that is more amazing than the next person.

The way comparison tries to rob me of joy is through the other pastors that I follow which are the same age as me. I keep seeing their posts and the services they run and the impact they make in their communities and Satan whispers, "You should be further along by now." It seems like with every step you take you find a whole new set of people that are doing that thing that you are doing but only like a million times better. The difference is that it didn't take them nine million years to get fifty followers on their podcast. As a preacher, comparison follows you before every sermon you preach and with our access to amazing preachers from every crevice of the planet, it follows you after you're done too.

So how do we snap out of this cycle that ungodly ambition can set us on and what does godly ambition even look like?

I believe if we were honest—like I mean, really honest about our lives—it would help others see behind this curtain. Sometimes people need to see how the sausage is made, or maybe more accurately, we need to allow them to visit the Chipotle of our lives. What I mean by that is at

Chipotle you can see clearly how your food is being made. We need people to see more than just the finished product, thus creating a narrative that is actually realistic. It would also help if we lived our best moments in the moment and actually thought about not just our own fulfillment, but also had in mind the possible discontentment we may cause in others. You may say life is too short to think about how others may feel but that is not biblical at all. Life is too short to not consider others. I love how Romans 14:13-22 talks about this.

3 Therefore let us not pass judgment on one another any longer, but rather decide never to put a stumbling block or hindrance in the way of a brother. 14 I know and am persuaded in the Lord Jesus that nothing is unclean in itself, but it is unclean for anyone who thinks it unclean. 15 For if your brother is grieved by what you eat, you are no longer walking in love. By what you eat, do not destroy the one for whom Christ died. 16 So do not let what you regard as good be spoken of as evil. 17 For the kingdom of God is not a matter of eating and drinking but of righteousness and peace and joy in the Holy Spirit. 18 Whoever thus serves Christ is acceptable to God and approved by men. 19 So then let us pursue what makes for peace and for mutual upbuilding.

20 Do not, for the sake of food, destroy the work of God. Everything is indeed clean, but it is wrong for anyone to make another stumble by what he eats. 21 It is good not to eat meat or drink wine or do anything that

causes your brother to stumble. 22 The faith that you have, keep between yourself and God. Blessed is the one who has no reason to pass judgment on himself for what he approves. 23 But whoever has doubts is condemned if he eats, because the eating is not from faith. For whatever does not proceed from faith is sin.

The encouragement I find from this passage when I look at our world of constant discontentment and unrealistic timelines on social media is that we should actually be aware of what we are projecting to people who may be in a tough place. We shouldn't put anything in the way of another that may cause them to stumble or lose sight of Jesus.

A few years back I remember going on Instagram and looking on my timeline at all the Christian artists and pastors I was following. I wanted to see how many of them were encouraging me to follow Jesus and how many were causing me to want to be more selfish. It was actually a very discouraging exercise. I was bombarded by posts of high-end fashion purchases and an endless supply of look-how-awesome-I-am posts. A very small percentage of those posts were reaching out or sharing a truth from God's Word that didn't have them also making much of themselves. These are the people I would have said were the most well-known followers of Christ at the time.

Now it may have just been purely coincidental—perhaps just a set of bad days where everyone was on the wrong track. But something was telling me that God wanted to show me the great disparity between the people He shows me in His Word and the people who I look at on my phone. A year later an Instagram account called "PreachersNSneakers" popped up and, despite my feelings about what an account like that can do to the body of Christ, it highlights the exorbitant gloating that is so often going on. Now don't hear what I'm not saying. I'm not saying that if you buy high-end clothing then you're not an effective pastor or posting about lunch with your girl-friends at Nobu isn't being a good steward. I'm saying that if you're a Christian leader you need to have a greater awareness of allowing your life to show how the things of this world should grow strangely dim in the light of God's glorious grace.

A few days after this experience I remember getting a call from a friend asking if I wanted to meet Francis Chan. He was having breakfast with a few pastors in the area before speaking at a conference and this guy said I had a seat if I wanted it. I gladly said yes! I had the day all planned with how I was going to ask Francis to take a photo with me holding my book. The caption was ready —"Fran (that's what his friends call him) and I, having a chat about my book." I mean I knew that in the world of social media the picture would look like this man and I were a lot closer than we really were. Then minutes before it was time to get this epic picture taken the Holy Spirit convicted me.

"Don't even take the picture."

"What? Do you know who this is?" I asked, as though

the Holy Spirit hasn't read *Crazy Love*! This was an opportunity, man! In the world, perception is reality, and if people perceive that I hang out with the big dogs maybe I myself will be a big dog. I was totally ignoring what Jesus said to His disciples concerning the big dogs of His day.

Anyway the conviction didn't leave. "Don't take the picture, Rob," I kept reminding myself. Have you ever seen a kid throwing a tantrum in a toy store or, better yet in a restaurant, and the parents have to drag the kid out kicking and screaming? That picture was the internal battle happening the whole time I was waiting to speak to Francis Chan. Why do I think this happened in this way? To be honest I have no clue. But if I were to guess, I would say after everything that God had shown me that week, He didn't want me to be a part of that social media "oh look at me" circus. "Rob, is knowing me and being known by me enough for you?" Yes, Jesus. It is.

I believe that day He wanted me to be different, not *better*, but different. He didn't want one of my friends in ministry to see my picture and think to themselves, "Geez look at Rob, he's going places, having breakfast with Francis Chan." That wouldn't be the real story, yet it may cause significant discontentment in someone else's heart. Now since that day I've met people and posted cool pictures with very little context. I have since then succumbed once in a while to the low-hanging fruit of looking better than I really am. I know that not every situation requires the same obedience but that day I needed to be especially aware of my situation. We can't constantly live in a space of also not enjoying something because we are worried what people will think if it wasn't a conviction we felt in that moment. We have to be sensitive to God's leading in our endeavors and all that entails.

Comparison is a thief. Call it what you want but it is the root of multiple sad endings. When we live in a world of constant comparison we only manifest selfish ambition and chasing that means we never get to godly ambition. So what is godly ambition? What is healthy ambition? I believe that whatever you do, if your heart is fully in it to glorify God and it aligns with what God is about, then go for it. Yes, sure, times will come where your heart will try its level best to distort that and put you on the glory seat again, but that's when you go back to the drawing board and course correct. Our hearts must be fixed on the greater prize and our identity has got to be secure in whose we are. My wife is always saying that to me! Whose are you? Always be secure in whose you are and you'll always be cool with who you are!

See, that's what Paul says is the secret to being content —realizing that you were bought with a great price and claimed by a King who gave His all for you! That is some pretty reassuring stuff right there!

THE HYPE

There is a famous illustration of a sports player who worked hard all their life to win a championship and finally when they got the prize they worked so hard to get—once the trophy is finally in their hands—they find they aren't as satisfied as they thought they would be. They're empty. The trophy didn't promise the fulfillment they thought it would bring. I don't know how true that illustration is because I've never been there but I have had dreams come true only to find out in the moment that the dream wasn't all that it was made out to be.

Growing up in Africa, all we ever wanted was to come to America. I mean, with each episode of T.R.L we were sold that this was the place where every dream came true. The United States was the promised land where suffering didn't exist, Mickey Mouse and 50 Cent were next door neighbors, and there was this burger that could fulfill your every desire called a Big Mac!

I remember coming over in 2006 for the very first time. We arrived at L.A.X with our dreams and a cardigan (no kidding). When I came to the States I was literally an opening line in a Miley Cyrus song about the U.S.A. The first thing I noticed was how ordinary everyone's clothes were. No chains, no cool gear—I mean no one had a pair of Jordans on! I couldn't help but be smacked in the face by the big difference from the America I had seen on my T.V in Zimbabwe to the America I could see, feel, touch and (certainly in some places as we drove to the house from the airport) smell!

I saw destitute people and beggars, driving through some pretty rough looking areas during our two week stay. These places were certainly rougher than any I had ever seen near my middle-class suburban upbringing in Harare.

On the flip side, we also saw some pretty wealthy and unbelievable places not too far from the abject poverty. I couldn't quite fathom this and yet this had always been the America that existed. This was me now seeing the whole picture and not a snippet of the America on the silver screen. Not everyone was happy and wealthy in this place even though the hype was saying otherwise.

This is the hype behind ambition. We see a startup tech company blow up and think, "Wow I want that." We see the sold out concerts and the fancy cars and private jets and we Bow Wow Challenge our way to that place of false fulfillment, selling the brochure to the next person. When you get to the top you realize that it may not be lonely, as Drake would say, but there is more hype for you and a whole bunch of people selling the next mountaintop experience. It's like climbing an endless Everest that will give you no rest at all and every time you look like you've reached the summit you find there is way more climbing to do that requires better gear and more expensive guides. The hype in ambition has no end. Hype just begets more hype and never fulfills.

THE HOPE

You are enough. Like right now, as you are. No additional side hustle to complete you. No need for that extra hundred followers to make you feel like somebody. You *are* somebody. I am a pastor and I'm telling you that there are a bunch of people even in my line of work who should be the most content ever yet don't buy the hope. They're all in on the hype. Even in our godly pursuits we are like Jesus' brothers in John 7:3-5 encouraging Him to get to the big cities to make a greater impact.

Jesus' brothers said to him, "Leave Galilee and go to Judea, so that your disciples there may see the works you do. No one who wants to become a public figure acts in secret. Since you are doing these things, show yourself to the world." For even his own brothers did not believe in him.

Jesus' brothers, who didn't even believe in Him, misread His mission and thought it was about being bigger and more famous. They wanted to build some hype around Jesus, but Jesus didn't respond the way they think and believe He should have. Jesus wasn't about being more famous for fame's sake. He was about heavily investing in the few in order to reach the many, and we misread this godly ambition and become a people and a church that is about the *crowds*. We gotta trust that if we just follow faithfully the moment will present itself at just the right time. Godly ambition requires a lot of patience and a lot of faith. We're in it for the sake of Christ and whether our name is recognized or not we will see it through to the end.

There is a game called Jenga where the goal is to remove pieces without the whole structure collapsing. Our lives should have moveable pieces but the piece that will bring the whole structure down should always be Jesus. We have to make sure that Jesus is the bottom piece that everything is built on—the cornerstone of our lives. We need to make sure we are not putting Jesus on the second or third floor but rather asking Jesus to be the immovable piece in our lives. If Jesus is not at the centre of our lives then someone or something else is.

I am still battling with this even as I write this line. Is what I'm writing smart enough? Is this the best way to put that? I mean Jenga, Rob? You're gonna give an illustration of Jesus in Jenga? I am being almost way too honest with this book but I believe that when writing this chapter and calling it "This may not be about Jesus" I'm confessing and asking Jesus to make it about Him. I don't want to stay in the shallow end of endless posts about empty successes or the hamster-cycle thingy of looking for affirmation. I want to be found rooted in the hope that is never changing, for ever and ever. So stuff it! So what if you don't think these words are the greatest thing you've ever heard? I have gotta say it until I believe it and even more—until I live it!

We all need love. We all need affection and, to some degree, attention. My challenge to us and yes, you read that right—I'm included here—is this: That we become individuals that find our significance in Christ. My hope is that we will no longer have to write, preach or live our lives in a vicious cycle of chasing the significance we already have in Christ. Pastors will just be themselves and not have to cut their jeans and wear Chelsea boots in order to reinvent themselves for a people that just need authentic community. Worship leaders would lead worship as worshippers, not as performers who are seeking to live their unfulfilled rock star dream through their ministry. My prayer is that through this book you would see my own life as an honest, open book that probably doesn't have most of the answers but may carry some. I say this because I feel it; I can sense the yearning in my heart to chase after something I was never meant to chase after.

To the cool pastor movement, this chapter may have sounded like a rebuke to you at some point but that's not my heart. Be the you Christ has made you to be. To the Old Navy, boot cut jeans, white New Balance wearing pastors out there, you too! Don't do whatever it takes to get in, you're already in! You are the you that God needs you to be. Authenticity is the constant in genuine godly ambition. You are loved beyond measure and called to do this thing whether you're in a stadium full of people or a tiny living room trying to make disciples. We have the same audience at all times and that is Jesus.

One of my leaders once said this and it hit my heart so hard: "When Jesus looks at our gatherings, He doesn't use a calculator to count numbers but He uses a scale to weigh how much of Him our gatherings carry. We're there for Him and everyone should all be there for Him and never us."

To you, yes you wherever you stand: if you're being called to sell lipstick that doesn't come off then do it for His glory and chase that with a heart that is rooted in Christ. Keep telling yourself that you're enough. Maybe you're working toward being the C.E.O someday, then keep going for it. Top of your class, go for it! Do it for His glory and never because you don't feel like you're enough because you. Are. ENOUGH.

Three final things I want to leave you with when it comes to ambition.

1. Check your motive.

2. Is it taking you away from Jesus?

3. Is it making you a "me monster"?

I know God is asking me the questions that I'm asking you to ask yourself. Am I chasing my own significance in Jesus' name? Am I missing out on being content with what God has given me? Am I using my gift to glorify Him? To make much of Him alone?

Finally this: Does my life and entire existence make absolutely no sense if Jesus is removed? If not, then is He truly my foundation or just the expendable Jenga piece?

SEX

"I don't think I can marry her," Jim muttered to himself, sitting in his driveway with his head in his hands.

It was 2am. Jim had just come back from dinner with his fiancé, Kerry. Their night started off as a well-intentioned wedding-planning date complete with a wonderful home-cooked meal, but it ended up with Jim and Kerry having sex, again.

Riddled with guilt, Jim was turning to his go-to excuse —blaming it on Kerry. "If only she were more spiritual," he thought. "Is she even the one?"

He thought, again, about his recent graduation from seminary and how he just landed a position as a youth pastor at a local church. That all just added to the weight of shame.

"I always say I'll never be here again," he thought, "but I find myself right back at square one time and time again. Will it end?"

Jim was a typical twenty-seven-year-old. He had a crummy apartment which was never tidy, with Xbox controllers lying around everywhere and day-old uncleaned cereal bowls on his kitchen counter. Only a few months were left before getting hitched but this roller coaster of emotions, swaying from looking forward to marriage and then feeling tremendous guilt over sex, was spiritually exhausting. He really loved Jesus but couldn't understand why he didn't love Him enough to honor him with purity. Why couldn't he simply say "we need to stop!" when things got heated with Kerry?

I don't know if you can think of a similar situation for yourself. Maybe you're even living in it right now. Maybe you're not trying to be a youth pastor but everyone at work knows that you're a Christian and you feel like a complete phony. I've seen this scenario time and time again where couples feel so guilty about their sexual mistakes that they altogether stop pursuing Jesus. Guys stop leading spiritually because they feel they don't have any spiritual credibility left, and women start to feel like they're dirty in the eyes of God.

Jim and Kerry's story is a made-up one, but only just. On one hand it is such a familiar story in the circles I have been in as a young adults pastor, and on the other it sounds a lot like my own story. The story of people that are so broken because they love God but keep on falling into the same trap over and over again—people who keep on failing sexually in their earnest pursuit of Jesus.

There is a direct correlation between sex and guilt in

most Christian circles. It's something that destroys so many relationships in our communities. And yet, despite the prevalence of sex, it's still one of those things we don't talk about often enough. When it comes to sexuality and biblical marital parameters, yes, the Church loves talking about that. But sex and healthy sexuality—not so much! It may be because we are fearful that no matter how well-intentioned our attempts at bringing life to people in this area, we may just end up being mocked in a Relevant magazine post ten years from now.

So why is it so difficult to accurately and proportionally broach the topic of sex and Christianity? Well I believe it might be because sex and sexuality have been so distorted in the world we live in that we may no longer be totally convinced that it's a good, God thing. Sex is good and sex is God's gift to us.

We'll pause right there for now.

SEXY NEVER REALLY LEFT

God created sex. He owns the patent on it. He knows how it's meant to be. He wants you to have it. Just in the way He says it is best enjoyed.

There is this company I bring up over and over again because they are the epitome of hype. Supreme is a billion dollar brand that is exclusive as heck (ah, Christian curse words). It is next to impossible to get an original Supreme anything at retail, and because of this it means there are tons of knock-offs in the market. The most recent one was a knock-off flagship store launched in Shanghai, China. This store is insanely cool and features architectural design that is delectable to the eye, and even an indoor skate park among many other cool things, but... it still isn't the real things—it's still a knock-off store! They spent all that time and money and creativity to create something that is a knock-off. So naturally, they are getting sued by the original Supreme because you can't just make someone else's store and sell fake stuff with their brand name on it. I understand why they did it but it doesn't make it okay. See, there is high demand for Supreme clothing or anything with branding on it but there is very little supply. This means that there is so much money to be made if you can make a good fake.

There are funny parallels I can draw between Supreme and sex. There is constant hype around Supreme just like there is with sex. I mean since the beginning of time, sex has had hype over and over again. If sex could only be found in ten stores around the world like Supreme, there would be people lined around blocks upon blocks outside to access it. Sex is exclusive! God made it that way. Demand will always be way more than supply. Many will catch L's (losses) trying to pursue both, but unlike James Jebbia, the founder of Supreme, the creator of sex actually wants you to have it.

So God created mankind in his own image, in the image of God he created them; male and female he created them.

28 God blessed them and said to them, "Be fruitful and increase in number; fill the earth and subdue it. Rule over the fish in the sea and the birds in the sky and over every living creature that moves on the ground." (Genesis 1:27-28)

Right out the gate after God makes Adam and Eve, He drops command number one—have sex! Literally! In His plan He created sex to be enjoyed. He is all for it to be had and He doesn't beat around the bush about it. He says go for it—as often as you can, too! Later God would give someone the knowledge to create Tylenol so that headaches can't even stop it from happening anymore! He is all for it and we need to preach and teach that more and more. He doesn't see anything wrong with a lot of bump and grind.

But our Supreme store in Shanghai has one more problem. If you buy something in that store you will always know that it isn't the real deal. You will always look like you have a Supreme shirt but in your heart of hearts you will never know what a real Supreme shirt feels like. You literally will never fully enjoy what you have. On the other hand, can you imagine being James Jebbia, the founder of Supreme, and seeing your hard work ripped off just like that?

Imagine it—making something and designing it and then some dude steals your idea, bootlegs it, and claims that it's the real deal. That's what Satan did with sex. Adam and Eve were hooked up with twenty-four hour nakedness and a lifetime (and lifetimes were long back then) with the hottest dude and girl on the planet, no questions asked. Libido on fleek, never having to pop a pill that's on a commercial with two people in separate bathtubs. Just sex, wilderness and more sex. That was what God gave them. And just in case they didn't get the memo He makes it clear, "Hey yo, get it on!" (message trap remix version).

Look, I know this is nothing new and that every Christian book on marriage, dating and sex is going to say this but the reason why this must be reiterated again and again is because Satan's version of what he stole is constantly advertised as being the better version. He has created a lot of hype around a complete fake. Our greatest problem is we don't read the fine print on the label. In God's version His mission statement is, "Life and life to the full", but Satan's is, "Steal, kill and destroy." (John 10:10.)

Sex, when placed in the wrong space, is devastating. Instead of being a beautiful picture of the coming together of two people who've said they love each other and are never leaving each other, it becomes, "Hey can I use you for ten minutes, two days or even two months of pleasure and never see you again?" Without the commitment God set in place for it to flourish, it's destructive and fake, no matter how you chop it up.

As an African in his mid-30's I'm all too familiar with Satan's plan for sex outside of marriage. I saw a nation, or dare I say an entire continent, get destroyed by AIDS. A disease that is sexually transmitted was the perfect storm for the enemy to reveal the great difference between his plan and God's plan. Thousands died and many children were left orphaned. There was a time where one in every four children in Zimbabwe was an orphan due to AIDS. This disease drastically decreased the life expectancy in Zimbabwe and at its peak that number had been reduced to thirty-two years. Can you imagine that? Growing up in a place where you were only expected to live to thirty-two?

Here is the kicker. All people had to do was remain faithful to one another and the disease would be eradicated. Even though there was a massive campaign encouraging the use of condoms, there's still a risk even if you use them. I personally remember a two year period where I basically attended a funeral every two months to bury a close relative who had been taken by this disease. It was horrifying, living with some of your closest friends and family, watching them walk the most painful, dehumanizing ending to life you can imagine—attending a funeral and looking at the spouse of a loved one knowing that this will be them in a few months. Satan's full blown plan for sex was exposed for all of us to see.

PORN AND SEX TRAFFICKING

Here are some stats from conquerseries.com:

• The porn industry's annual revenue is more than the NFL, NBA, and MLB combined.

• It is also more than the combined revenues of ABC, CBS, and NBC.

- 47% of families in the United States reported that pornography is a problem in their home.

Pornography use increases the marital infidelity rate by more than 300%.

- 11 is the average age that a child is first exposed to porn, and 94% of children will see porn by the age of 14.
- 55% of married men and 25% of married women say they watch porn at least once a month.
- 68% of church-going men and over 50% of pastors view porn on a regular basis.
- Of young Christian adults 18-24 years old, 76% actively search for porn.

Pornography is everywhere and this distorted view of sex is shaping a generation in ways that we are oblivious to. I don't know about you but those stats are jarring, and if they don't gut us to the core then I'm afraid Satan has won the battle of desensitization. We conceal this thing and make it almost impossible for people who are struggling with this highly addictive sin to break out of it. There is not nearly enough openness and honesty around it especially from the over fifty percent of pastors who wrestle with this sin. I opened this chapter with a story of a guy sleeping with his fiancé but there is no doubt in my heart that the root of that situation is what we allow to enter our hearts through our eyes.

34 Your eye is the lamp of your body. When your eye is

healthy, your whole body is full of light, but when it is bad, your body is full of darkness. (Luke 11:34)

We have to be aware of what we are letting into our souls and how that is doing damage to our hearts. Our innermost being is being attacked and we are willing to let that which is most precious be invaded. I once heard my good friend, Simon share in a video how we are so diligent in making sure our homes are protected. We lock them up when we leave, we install security alarms on our doors to make sure that no one can get in, and yet we don't do that for our soul. If there is a challenge in this chapter it is this: no matter how young or old you are, purity is still a thing to God. He wants us to guard that.

By far the most damaging stat about porn is that only seven percent of pastors say their church has a program to help people struggling with it. Think of all that porn does and more, then think of what seven percent looks like. It is a drop in the ocean in a world that is driving eleven-year-olds to something so dark. I think that there is no way that stat could be right. My daughter can't possibly be exposed to the darkness that porn is in nine years. I pray that she never has to lay eyes on things I regret seeing.

The anger that God must have toward Satan. I can't imagine that kind of wrath welling up in the heart of love itself. I feel it welling up inside me as I write this. There are women who are trafficked, girls who never get to see the light of day, evil men who get eighteen-year-olds hooked on heroin, drugging up girls as we fuel this slavery with every click. It is utter bull to think that there is such a thing as ethical porn. Excuse my anger but it is infuriating to think that Satan gets away with this fake crap.

We as followers of Christ have been given a mandate to push back what is dark in this world; to redeem and restore what was stolen by the enemy and to point God's creation back to Him; to take sledge hammers to the evil that exploits the innocent and bash down that bootleg flagship store and point people to the real thing! To give hope instead of the hype! And to start doing this, let's believe the hope for ourselves and see through the hype!

There are three things I wish I would have asked or received regarding sex and sexuality when I was younger. Perhaps you resonate with these.

1. I WISH I HAD "THE TALK", BUT IT DOESN'T HAPPEN IN SHONA FAMILIES.

How did I find out about sex? I stumbled upon an adult magazine in a closet when I was eight-years-old and I had no idea what I was looking at. There I was, a kid looking at some random woman standing naked, and immediately I knew there was something wrong. I knew I wasn't meant to be looking at it, that there was something sacred and secret about it. There was an innocence in me that was being snatched away by looking at an image which was suggesting something beyond what my little mind could fathom.

I remember for years when I was bored I would run to

this closet and peek again, and with each peek that inno-cence in me kept dying. It looked like the older I got the more I wanted to go back to this closet. So as I grew up I eventually found myself at an all-boys high school where the more you knew about sex the more impressive you were. Pornography, which is illegal in Zimbabwe, became what weed is in an American high school. Guys would bring magazines and tapes wrapped up in newspapers and would circulate pornographic material to be shared and traded.

So my first talk was no talk at all. It wasn't with my brother. It wasn't with someone who cared about me, but rather it was a video tape that shocked the life out of me and made the magazine in the closet look like nothing compared to this. It went from zero to sixty as soon as I popped that tape into the VHS player at home.

This started years of struggling with porn and lust to a point that there are times in my life where I felt like the most revolting thing alive. The images I saw of pleasure and the result of seeing HIV and AIDS rip through people I love were oxymoronic. I remember thinking to myself, is this what women are like? Is this how women want to be treated? Everything about my first encounters with porn have revealed just how evil that industry is in taking the place of an extremely important conversation that parents need to have with their children. Until this day I have never had a healthy conversation about sex with someone that I felt safe with and thought I could ask questions. It's too taboo in church to have these candid talks and it's important to note that even Adam and Eve had the talk with God first. Our Heavenly Father doesn't run away from it but He confronts it head on with no shame. Parents—there is no shame in beating porn to the punch when it comes to having conversations about sex.

So I never had the talk with my parents and I think that's mainly because it is by far the most culturally taboo thing to do. This may also be the reason why so many people were destroyed by AIDS where I'm from. The male and female reproductive organs' scientific names are curse words in my language. Can you imagine it being a swear word to just say "penis" or "vagina"? Now try and imagine how a talk that has those two words being said repeatedly would play out. I also wonder if there may have been some pride or even shame around my parents' own sexual journey as well. I know it's going to be so hard for me to share my mistakes with my kids around this subject when the time comes. It's hard to tell love stories that have beginnings with sexual mistakes and some bad judgement calls in them. I know that is part of my journey too, which is why I hope to be bold and brave in talking to my children about those beginnings with every hope that they wouldn't walk the road I walked. They may some day sit in a service and hear me talk about sex to a church, or maybe even have some impressions of how their mom and I are actually attracted to each other in that way. Gross for the kiddos I know, so I apologize Hope and Nik Nak whenever you read this! My prayer is that they will hear about sex enough times from us in an intimate, private, and safe setting before they hear it in a public context or read it in a book. I have made so many mistakes and have also seen the God-glorifying side of this gift that I must be intentional about being in community with people in different stages of life to teach and learn about sex.

> Teach the older men to be temperate, worthy of respect, self-controlled, and sound in faith, in love and in endurance. 3 Likewise, teach the older women to be reverent in the way they live, not to be slanderers or addicted to much wine, but to teach what is good. 4 Then they can urge the younger women to love their husbands and children, 5 to be self- controlled and pure, to be busy at home, to be kind, and to be subject to their husbands, so that no one will malign the word of God. 6 Similarly, encourage the young men to be self-controlled. 7 In everything set them an example by doing what is good. In your teaching show integrity, seriousness (Titus 2:2-7)

In this passage in Titus you see the principle of cross-generational community. Without losing focus by the particulars that may be slightly controversial, the main principle is one we should grab a hold of and never let go. Mentorship and cross-generational community is a key building block in breaking sexual strongholds in the generations to come. The talk is important!

I still wish I had it. I still wish there were more older men and women who loved God and honored sexual purity

—men and women who were willing to be vulnerable and real and are invested in debunking myths surrounding sex, especially in a Christian marriage. Before I was married my mind had been so messed up by all the junk my brain had downloaded over the years that I wasn't even sure if "Christian sex" was good! I'm just being real! I also can't believe I said Christian sex! Like what does that even mean? Do we have Kumbaya playing to set the mood in the background instead of Boyz 2 Men? These are real feelings people have though and there is no one to talk to about it. I mean, if the difference between excitement level is the same as the one between a Steven Curtis Chapman concert or a Travis Scott concert (or Luke Bryan if that's your cup of tea) then we will always buy the lie. Unless of course you're hyped about Steven Curtis Chapman which some people are! I mean heck, I might choose the latter myself if it's framed that way.

We have to be real. Authentic Christian community allows you to peek behind the curtain of each others' lives. The Bible is ridiculously real. It allows us to see the people who love God on the mountain top but it also lets us see them looking at a woman bathing on the roof. It is real!

2. WAS I BORN LIKE THIS? WILL MY DESIRE TO HOOK UP EVER GO AWAY?

Sexuality is complicated. I'm not a sexologist or sex therapist, so I gladly stay in my lane, which comprises of my own personal experience. For me, I battled with wondering when I would get over the desire to want what I shouldn't want, and hoped for the day when I wouldn't have to fight for every yard in my pursuit for sexual purity. I had been downloading all these images and sexual encounters for decades before I started walking with Jesus. Then the journey with Jesus started and some things seemingly disappeared instantly while others lingered and kept knocking on the door of my soul. Lust chose to stay. It simply didn't want to leave my life.

Eventually I started asking myself: was I born like this? Am I genetically predisposed to want something that God doesn't want for me? If there is something in me banging on the door of my soul saying, Rob, you gotta have sex with every beautiful woman that walks this planet, who put it there? Why would God make me super heterosexual if He didn't want me to pounce on every beautiful woman that has a pulse? Left to my own devices and submitting to the part of me that wants nothing to do with Jesus I would be free to just do who I'm made to be, right? Isn't it just easier to do whatever appears to come most naturally?

"I was born this way, so then it must be okay" is not a good argument for giving into something that's not honoring to God. I also can't look to culture, which gives me the green light to accept my desires, even if that culture or community is claiming to let me do this in Jesus' name. If I just found women that were cool with sleeping with me and my wife was okay with it and everything was consensual, it would *still* be wrong—even if I wasn't obviously hurting anyone.

My particular genetic predisposition actually finds its

home in a sect of Christianity that believes in Christian polyamory. Yes, there are Christians who believe that polyamorous relationships are not ungodly. If you are not familiar with what polyamory is then let me explain. Polyamory means that as long as it is all consensual between the parties involved and nobody is getting hurt, it's okay to love and have sexual relations with multiple people. This is different from polygamy. Polygamy is a type of marriage that almost always involves a man taking on multiple wives, but polyamory is more inclusive and far more egalitarian. I'll talk about this more in chapter 7 when we deal with sexual identity, so keep this thought in your back pocket.

But the reason why I mention this now is to note that I can easily find a place, and theology, that backs up my desires. Just google what you're looking for, and bam! you can find a community and a movement and theology--usually revolving around Paul's 'cultural context' or some other complicated argument--that validates your desires and provides you the excuses you're hoping to find. I'm not the only one with these desires. You can find a hype to suit your desires, but it's just a fake.

I don't have to wonder if I'm born this way, I already know that most men are. Pornography is the most socially accepted pluralistic sexual experience and it wouldn't make the amount of money it makes if it were not true. But if in our sinful nature we gravitate to more than one sexual partner, is it okay to go ahead just because we feel we were born that way? But, were you really born that way? And can these desires really ever go away?

The answer to the first question is yes. Yes you were born like this. There are many explanations for the vices we gravitate toward. Some are genetic and some are just feelings we can't explain away. Did I find that magazine at eight-years-old or did it find me? Was it my fault? Did God not know that this would scar me and plague me for years after being exposed to it? Some questions seem unanswered, and will only frustrate you. But throwing verses at the origin of your sin or the difficulty of what you carry isn't really what we are looking for when we ask these questions. God doesn't make mistakes. Genesis gives us a glimpse at two bros that were born in the same family and are the first siblings on the scene. Life is all good until jealousy and envy come into the picture. Cain busts his way into the biblical narrative and just like that here comes the hot stepper, a murderer. Cain didn't have to learn murder, he just did it. Adam didn't teach him to murder, right? So what was that? The evolution of anger gave birth to murder. Cain's answer to his lack of affirmation from God was to murder the one to whom the affirmation had been given. These particular verses in Genesis chapter 4 are important here.

6 Then the Lord said to Cain, "Why are you angry? Why is your face downcast? 7 If you do what is right, will you not be accepted? But if you do not do what is right, sin is

crouching at your door; it desires to have you, but you must rule over it." (Genesis 4:6-7)

God intervenes before the disaster and warns Cain to cool down. He actually directs him to life. He tells Cain in his state of brokenness where sin is to be found, what it wants from him, and what he must do when it knocks.

God doesn't make mistakes, only masterpieces. Because of sin we are pretty much born into a world that pulls us toward sin and away from Him at each opportunity. God loves us enough to search for us and lead us to life. Cain may have been born with anger issues and parents who amplified that by constantly reminding one another about who ate the fruit which put them in the mess they were in, but God still made a way. God still reached out to him before his anger turned to sin, before his identity issues and performance-driven affirmation led him to murder.

God knows the broken bits of us, each and every one of them. He knows what amplifies that brokenness. But I believe that God searches so completely for us with truth and warning to better inform us of the right decision to make when the time comes. I've learned that I need to give my desires to God. I have to allow Him to be my master which means I surrender to what He says and I trust what He says; that I lean on the Word more than my own under-standing; and that in my weakness His power is made perfect.

We may live hoping that we will someday all be restored

to factory settings, but God actually says He is replacing the entire system. He promised a new heaven and a new earth and that is what we get to look forward to. Even though I'm messed up and still a work in progress, I'm not looking for people who think that loving me means they accepting my sin and give me justification for it, but rather people who are leading me to a God who wants to give me life and acceptance. A God who says, Yes Rob, you were born that way, but just like Jesus said to Nicodemus — you gotta be born again. In September 1983 I was born with a fracture that led me to just desire the side of sex that is self-seeking, but in July 2007 I was born again into a being that can now see this brokenness and desires to be led to the God-glorifying version of sex - who desires the real, not the fake; the hope, not the hype.

3. WHAT IS THE POINT OF WAITING?

We love asking this question, don't we? The answer here is both easy and difficult. The intimacy between a man and a woman is the most intimate connection there can be between two people. This special, sensual, spiritual, pleasurable and so-much-more thing is the thing God created to solidify the bond between a man and a woman. But there is more: God created this as the means to bring kids into this world. Sex is also multiplication! It produces beautiful fruit.

I have to be sensitive to the fact that I know some married couples who can't have kids are reading this, and sex hasn't produced that for you. I don't know your pain but I do know that there is a brokenness in the world we live in that I have no answers for. In those moments I just pray and trust God's plan for you and cling to the knowledge of His love.

For those with kids, you know there is no person you ever love that much before even knowing them. This is the beauty of something that sex was created to do. Adam made love to his wife and Cain was born. So to say we should guard sex and be protective of who we share this bond with is not even doing justice to how sacred this act is. If there is one thing that I have ever done that leads me to a place of saying to God how awesome He is, it's having sex in a marital context. Before I was married, sex was like the fake Supreme, it had an element of emptiness or guilt associated with it right after, but in marriage... man, oh man, God is good!

But what if sex sucks in marriage and you only find this out after you've thrown a party that cost ten grand and on a vacation in a place you can barely afford?

These are the objections we hear. Shouldn't I have test-driven things before diving in? Well, let me attempt to answer that for you.

I hate flying. Well, hate is a strong word so let me rephrase that. I'm not *fond* of flying. Yes, I get that it's the safest way to get around but it also happens to be the one I am most uncomfortable with. The fact that you are in a tube with wings thousands of feet above the ground with zero chance of surviving a crash plays a big part in my lack of eagerness. The only reason I do fly is because it's efficient, fast and most importantly it comes with a high safety record. There is a one in eleven million chance that your plane will go down and, to put it in perspective, that is slightly lower than the odds of you ever winning the lottery. Yet we are so cautious when we get on a plane.

Now imagine an airline shrinking those odds and saying there is a fifty-fifty chance that you'll make it. Would you get on? Fifty-fifty odds are not good odds people, yet that's what happens when we get married. Some marriages are like Qantas, which is the safest airline and has never had a fatal crash; and some are like Air Zimbabwe, which, although never having a fatal crash, produce fear at every step of their ride. Their tag could easily be, "Air Zimbabwe: Where every bump feels like you're on your way to Jesus."

Because of these odds, which look more risky due to the high divorce rate (with reasons cited such as breakdown in relationship, lack of sexual compatibility, adultery), people think: Well, shouldn't I try rather before I buy? Isn't that safer? Why wait for marriage and go through all of this? Doesn't it make sense to have a couple of nights or days to make sure we are sexually compatible? Well, "try before you buy" makes sense if you are thinking that every breakdown in marriage is a result of bad sex. But actually, when you look at the details, you find the main reason why marriages break down is *because "try before you buy" is exactly what they did* - with a ton of people! They built into their lives a system and pattern of having way too many samples, like the dude who lingers in Costco all day trying each sample multiple times. There are people who have incredible sex lives who still get divorced, and I use the word "incredible" here knowing that an incredible sex life is a subjective thing.

But what if you knew why planes crashed and you could actually make sure the plane would make it? What if you could pick the pilot with the greatest safety record and the plane with the most efficient maintenance staff? If I could do that, I would get on a plane all day. If I just knew the pilot personally it would make a huge difference! Well, we can have that in our marriage. If God is the pilot and we follow His instructions to get the right people around our marriage we will see incredible change. God tells us that when He is at the center, things work. However, if *we* are at the center and our pleasure is the main point then it won't. In the Christian faith we have to establish one thing about how we do what we do - what the Bible says . We have to believe that as followers of Christ the Bible frames this for us in the New Testament repeatedly.

20 I have been crucified with Christ and I no longer live, but Christ lives in me. The life I now live in the body, I live by faith in the Son of God, who loved me and gave himself for me. (Galatians 2:20)

Those who belong to Christ Jesus have crucified the flesh with its passions and desires. (Galatians 5:24)

In those two passages, Paul gives us a framework for how we are no longer using the lens of our own satisfaction as the primary driver of the decisions we make. So in a nutshell, if God says so, then that really should be enough because He is the one steering the ship of our lives. It's always important to grasp the so-often missed reality that shouts loudest at us — *we have a master!* Surrender to Jesus!

SO LET ME CLARIFY A BIG THING.

The act of having sex may not be better just because you waited. We already live in such an oversexed culture where distorted views of sex are constantly floating around our brains even if we're virgins when we get married. I don't want you to read this and believe the act itself will be more enjoyable because you waited. It might be, but it also might not be. There is no science or measure available for anyone to say that. Your heart and soul will be in a place I can only hope I could've experienced and pray earnestly my children will someday experience; a place where you have nothing else to compare your spouse to; a place where sexual regret doesn't exist. For most married couples, good sex actually takes time—a long time of getting to know each other sexually. But the reason we wait is not because it will be more rewarding. The reason we wait is because it honors God and that is a big enough reason for someone who loves God. The reason why I don't cheat on my wife is not that sex with multiple people is not pleasurable, it is because I love her and I am honoring her. So the same with our love for God and our decisions to honor Him with our purity.

THE HYPE

Super Bowl Sunday 2018 and the Eagles are playing the New England Patriots. This could be the year they do it. Last play of the half goes down and the euphoria of seeing Nick Foles pull off the "Philly special" has us bouncing from wall to wall! But then, in a pure moment of watching a game that entire families have gathered around to root for their beloved team, sex pops up! Justin Timberlake is performing and our memories jog back to when Justin tried a little too hard to bring sexy back. What will my kids see if I step out of the room for a second? Maybe it's not Mr. Timberlake but rather some food commercial that decides that in order to stay in the headlines they need to do something more risqué?

These are genuine thoughts that are entertained in a moment that shouldn't have them, but we are living in an oversexed generation. I think we have to start right there. Who people choose to sleep with has become central to many debates and divisions all over the Western world. There is a rise in expectations of sexual performance too! Men in their 20's, 30's and 40's have started turning to impotence drugs so that they perform well. So much so that they have actually nicknamed top impotence drugs "the weekender" because they last for up to 36 hours in the bloodstream. Mainstream media and most social media platforms have successfully equated happiness in life with the amount of orgasms you can possibly pack in a lifetime.

So whether you're reading the comments on an ESPN

post on Instagram or watching a burger ad, sex is just around the corner. Sex sells and sex is always present. It is like the oxygen of our culture. This didn't start yesterday. It has been the norm for way longer than we realize. We have bought the fake Supreme version and we know it's not the real deal. We even built a store with a skatepark around our version of sex but it's not working out.

Outside of God's, and I reiterate, GOD'S PLAN, sex has become defined as nothing more than porn, abusive, trafficking, revengeful, a rebound, a 3-some, an orgy, premarital, a one-night stand, a hook-up. Where's the beauty in any of this? The list goes on. We are buying a lie and those lies range from "we all agree" to "we don't really"; from harmful to "who does it really harm?" Outside the knowledge of Christ your (fill in the blank) sex may not make sense as to why it's not part of God's plan, but whether you like it or not the hype is everywhere, and it is made up of nothing but thin air. The fallen version of sexuality is trying to pull us away from the full-bodied, beautiful redeemed version, and we judge others who struggle differently instead of seeing our own need for Christ's mercy, grace and love. Judgement should never be in the driver's seat when we are being missional. Truth, love, grace and mercy are what are on display. We are saved by grace and grace alone. We are inviting people to come and worship at the foot of the cross as broken people, not as already transformed. If we don't invite people as they are then we are being hypocritical of our own struggles. I can assure you there are people picketing against Pride rallies after a night of watching two women stuck in the abusive of porn having sex on a screen, on the very phone in their pockets. There are trains of thought that would claim that my sin is not as bad as yours. We can easily fall into the trap of thinking that the log in our eye is one God understands and is fine with. Buying into the hype can make us think that. The truth is we have all bought the hype to some extent and I will say again and again—hype has a shelf life.

THE HOPE

God didn't create sex so you can live in a cycle of guilt and shame. God certainly didn't create this beautiful thing to make you terrified of Him. He is the one who paid your debt and forgave you for your sin before you were even aware of it. He knows who you are, what you wrestle with, and has an amazing plan for your life if you choose Him. His grace and love is abundantly clear in His Word and through what He sent His one and only Son Jesus to accomplish on the cross. We have to be real so that we can be free to live a life where we are not anxiously waiting for the day our sexual life will be exposed and become a charge against us. If we pursue Him and all that He is, we will find that the more we love Him, the less we want other things. I lived for so long basing my Christianity on not being found out for what I was wrestling with, but I found it in wanting more of Christ than in having purity software installed on all my devices.

I have to confess, I still love Milli Vanilli. I mean I don't really care what you think of them but "their" songs were really catchy. If you don't know who they were, let me school you on them a little bit. Milli Vanilli was a German 90's pop group that took the world by storm. These black, dreadlocked, shoulder-pad-jacketed, cycling-pants-wearing RnB crooners sold tons of records and became super popular overnight. But no one including their fans were prepared for what was about to be discovered next. The duo had just won a Grammy Award when stories about lip syncing to other singers broke in a New York Times exposé. After initially denying it, the evidence became so overwhelming when a record skipped during a live performance, and their real voices were exposed. The world almost succinctly switched them off as the footage emerged of them scrambling on that MTV stage! In a time where social media didn't exist, this news travelled so quickly all over the world. It was unbelievable. "Girl you know it's true", a line from one of their most popular songs, was not quite as true as we all hoped. They had been exposed and the confessions quickly came rolling out. Before you could say *täuschen* ("deceive" in German) their Grammy and their top selling records were stripped from them.

When you follow Christ and struggle with sin, one of the biggest things that will weigh on you is when someone is going to find out. I call this the "Milli Vanilli" moment. God doesn't want us to live in the bondage of waiting for the moment everyone is going to find out that we're fakes but rather He wants us to live in freedom.

> Therefore, there is now no condemnation for those who are in Christ Jesus, 2 because through Christ Jesus the law of the Spirit who gives life has set you free from the law of sin and death. 3 For what the law was powerless to do because it was weakened by the flesh, God did by sending his own Son in the likeness of sinful flesh to be a sin offering. And so he condemned sin in the flesh, 4 in order that the righteous requirement of the law might be fully met in us, who do not live according to the flesh but according to the Spirit. (Romans 8:1-4)

Your heavenly Father already dealt with your shame and guilt by sending Jesus as an offering to pay the debt that you owe. So many of us live our entire lives as Christians thinking that Jesus is a referee waiting to throw a flag on every mistake that we are bound to make, but it's not the way He has set it up. God paid this huge ransom for us knowing that we would mess up time and again, so He set up a recurring payment called grace that makes sure that it's taken care of forever. Whatever your struggle is, God is aware of it already and He wants to walk with you through it. He comes to us before sin takes over like He did with Cain, and He shows us where the attack is coming from and how it can destroy us. He is ahead of it rather than shocked by it.

The real question Jim was asking at the beginning of

this chapter was, if I love Jesus why do I keep messing up? But maybe we should ask a different question. Maybe we should ask, if I love Jesus, why am I not running to Him in my moment of weakness and desperation? Why am I not leaning into the light with my relationship, my lust, my marital dissatisfaction, my attraction to people who are off limits, my brokenness and my guilt? His promise is freedom and the thing about freedom is this: If it doesn't feel like freedom, then it's not. But He has true freedom waiting for us!

RELATIONSHIPS

TINDER!!!

I'm shouting that out like they shout out "timber!" when a tree falls in a forest, to warn everyone that the tree is coming down. This is a warning that there isn't much of a judgement-free zone when it comes to that dating app in most Christian circles I've been in. I have observed the reality of someone confessing that they are on Tinder in a Christian group and you would have thought they were one of the hyenas from the Lion King daring to utter the word "Mufasa!". How could you use this abomination of a dating app that we're all pretty sure was invented to create a world of one-night stands at the mere swipe of a screen? Don't you know God has more for you? Someone call Hans Zimmer because we're going to need some pretty dramatic background music for what follows next!

I have been guilty of being in the don't-you-know-God-has-more-for-you squad. The problem is I have said those words in the comfort of my beautiful, secure, loving, guilt-free, sex-filled marriage vantage point. I realize now the error of my ways and publicly apologize to anyone I have said that to. The dating landscape has changed since the days of playing "Snake 2" on our Nokia 3310's. Let's just say the only "bumble boosting" going on in my 20's was going to multiple young adult groups on the same night.

ROMANTIC RELATIONSHIPS

I grew up in a time where one of the most insightful and impactful books on youth dating culture within the Church was, "I kissed Dating Goodbye" by Josh Harris. Now, I must say Josh has since kissed that book and Jesus goodbye but his book totally rocked an entire generation of Christian teens. Fast forward years later and the book has been picked apart, ridiculed, and I even heard a person say that it is the reason why there are so many divorces in that generation of Christians (which is really just an excuse for our own sinful nature). But "I Kissed Dating Goodbye" didn't make anyone get a divorce any more than "The Real Slim Shady" L.P. made people disrespect their moms.

Anyway, the book had a profound impact on Christian culture and was an antidote to the desperate cries in Christianity globally for dating clarity. So why do I bring this up? Our view of relationships as a culture inside and outside the church is constantly shifting. Josh's book went from being the most recommended book by youth pastors to the most criticized book by the same youth pastors who are now lead pastors. So in this ever changing world, what can we hold on to that is never changing?

Young people are more confused about what biblical dating and relationships should look like than when I was about what to do at a traffic circle in New Jersey. At least the latter can be googled. Have you ever tried to google and read all the articles on dating and relationships in the Church? Trust me, it is time consuming and you do not want to do that. Everyone seems to have an opinion or an angle on it and if you're reading this you're about to read mine, so buckle up.

The reason why I bring up Joshua Harris is because I can't think of a single person that made more of an impact on what I thought of dating and purity as a teenager. I mean geez, Josh had full access to form all my opinions because I had none. The opener of that book had me captivated and I wasn't as filled with guilt as some people were when reading his words. No, I was filled with encouragement. I wasn't going to mess up, I told myself, and I was going to have just one girl and only one that would line up next to me at that altar when it came time to say "I do". See, the amazing thing was that I was resonating with his message and I wasn't even a Christian at the time. I have a very complicated story as to how I became a follower of Christ, and I will spare the deets, but all that to say, there were some things in the book that just seemed right to me even though I wasn't even following Jesus.

The thing that made what Josh was saying (and still make it semi-bearable today) had to do with my Shona,

Zimbabwean culture. My culture, for the most part, believes and values the things Josh was celebrating in his book. Serial dating and playing the field are things that were already looked down upon when I was young, at least publicly. So here is the deal. If culture plays a part in how we read, receive and understand things in the Bible, then that has huge ramifications. If our culture esteems dating as an essential part of life, which most cultures around the world don't, then how do we find one message out of the Bible? How do we arrive at what God's plan is for this if we are all from different cultures? Take that a step further and you see that the culture the Bible is written in also makes it harder to establish a biblical baseline for this topic. Or does it? (If you're married and reading this, don't check out right now. There is more to this that filters into our marriages.)

So where is the dating book for our generation today? Where can we go to find a Josh Harris 2.0? My opinion is perhaps we don't need another dating book but need to figure out why we date and how that should lead us to God. If you're like me, you're consumed by doing the right thing. Maybe you don't want a line-up of girls standing next to you at the altar but your heart doesn't want the God who is able to transform your life either. That's where the conversation about relationships should start and end. God. Is He leading me and, if yes, what pleases Him when it comes to relationships, especially ones that are of a romantic nature?

MORE OR LESS DATING?

So what does the Bible say about dating? Well I would like to invite you to go to your Bible app and type "dating" in the search bar. You may as well type "Snapchat" in the bar because nothing will come up. Dating didn't exist in biblical times. In most cases, if not every case, you were only seen together in public after you were engaged to be married, and engagement looked quite different, too. Let's pause there. Back then, it could only be Facebook official if it was going to be marriage official. Now some of you reading this right now, if you're like me, will wonder how marriages even worked out back then, if this is the case. How could you meet someone and if you liked them you had to be instantly engaged? No time to be friends, no time to figure out if you both actually like The Office or Pad Thai noodles, just bam! We're getting married!

In some ways I think we have made an idol of our search for "the one". Some cultures don't even contemplate a world of choosing a spouse. Don't write this off but my wife and I joke around about how we are for arranged marriages—but we're only half joking. People marry people they didn't know all through history. It still happens in most of the world. Statistics show that 53.25 of marriages around the world are arranged. Yes, that's a real statistic. According to a survey conducted by Statistic Brain, the percentage of arranged marriages that end in divorce from this group are at 6.4 percent, and in India that rate drops to 1.2 percent.

I already told you about the 50 percent divorce rate that exists in America where we are knee deep in shows about people who get to take their pick from twenty guys at a time. Oh, let's not get into the whole fantasy suit deal. I don't have to wonder if God is cool with us being entertained by that. My hunch is absolutely not. Let me stop—I'm being judgey and I want my Bachelor friends to keep reading this so I'll pause there. But don't hear what I'm not saying either. Following Christ is not all about what we can and can't do but more about enjoying Him fully—being satisfied in Him so much that all we want to do is honor Him with every thought and action.

Dating is very much a cultural thing and mainly a Western one. In fact it wasn't really a thing until about a hundred years ago. Before then you couldn't really pick someone's daughter and take them somewhere unsupervised. So, as we in this society went from the gentleman caller to Tinder, how do we find the consistent hope in God's plan rather than getting swallowed up in the hype of our culture?

FINDING YOUR PERSON

I think we should start with where we all as Christians should be hoping a dating relationship will go. Marriage! Now obviously I am no love expert. In fact it is a miracle I ended up with my beautiful, precious wife. I remember the first time I told her I liked her. She almost sent me to the place where very few can come back from: the friend zone!

This is a hole that even Tom Brady can't crawl his way back from. Like seriously, Jesus saves but He doesn't help people get out of the friend zone. I have seen one too many guys being breadcrumbed in the friend zone for years watching endless reruns of Parks and Rec. This is a bonus tip to all the guys reading this: if she tells you about a guy she likes and says you give the best relationship advice, you're in The Zone. If it looks like you're in a Chevy commercial, then you're in a Chevy commercial—he who has ears to hear...

My (now, but not then) wife was starting to call me "bestie", and once you're a bestie you can forget "till death do us part"! I always raise my eyebrows whenever I hear a girl say she is marrying her best friend while she recites her vows. Lies! There is a real bestie, who proofread all the texts your fiancé sent you and stayed up with you till 4am every time you broke up with a guy. Now they're stuck in a friend zone warp they couldn't get out of and are currently crying in some far off place, while you say "I do!" So true and you know it ladies! I remember sitting in the car after another "hang out" time and I told her I liked her and there was a pause. She tried to slap the B.I.C. (brother in Christ) tag on me which is pretty much like when an N.F.L. team slaps the franchise tag on a player they are trying to keep and not pay.

Finally I maneuvered out of the pocket and got her to see me in a new light through some supernatural swagger-licious tactics. And here we are today, married for seven years. I may not be an expert on love and dating but I have thought long and hard about how to walk with young couples that are in that phase of life. I have found that life is found not in my own opinions but rather from drinking deeply from God's Word.

> But for Adam no suitable helper was found. 21 So the Lord God caused the man to fall into a deep sleep; and while he was sleeping, he took one of the man's ribs and then closed up the place with flesh. 22 Then the Lord God made a woman from the rib he had taken out of the man, and he brought her to the man.
>
> 23 The man said,
>
> "This is now bone of my bones
>   and flesh of my flesh;
> she shall be called 'woman,'
>   for she was taken out of man."
>
> 24 That is why a man leaves his father and mother and is united to his wife, and they become one flesh.
>
> 25 Adam and his wife were both naked, and they felt no shame. (Genesis 2:21-25)

Right out the gate in the creation story we see something cool happen. We see God creating everything in Genesis 1, and then God creates a man, Adam. Adam lands in this beautiful garden running buck naked and having just one job, naming things. I mean if you're reading this and you're a dude, you would agree that everything would be perfect except for the one thing that God wired Adam to know was missing: a beautiful woman!

So God gives Adam some Tylenol P.M and goes to work. When Adam opens his eyes, badabing, badaboom! He sees Eve for the first time. I mean Adam had seen every beautiful thing that had ever been created; he had named the most majestic of creatures; and in this moment he laid his eyes on something that caused him to say, "mine!"

There is a beautiful sequence when we look at that passage. This is the first couple in history. I mean everything is perfect at this point, right? So in a perfect world this is what the lead-up to marriage should look like. The first thing we see is that God is the cause of the situation. This is when God and His creation are in perfect relationship and Adam trusts God to truly provide whatever he needs. I always think about the things that God has caused in my life and how they have led to something beautiful that I was unaware God was preparing the whole time. Even as I write this, I know someone is going through a season of singleness and this quiet time is something God has caused in order to prepare you for something beautiful. So in your life, especially if you're single, my encouragement would be to never resent the season you're in. God might be causing something to happen that is ultimately for your good even if it doesn't lead to a relationship.

The next thing we see is that God does some pretty cool things that Adam was unaware of. I mean, God knew what Adam needed before Adam even knew it. He was the one who determined that there was no partner fit for him. God then designed Eve intricately from Adam's side. One thing I am so thankful for is that Adam didn't have a part in choosing what Eve would look like. Men all around the world are eternally thankful. God chooses Eve for Adam, making the very first relationship a match truly made in heaven and also an arranged marriage. Sleep, I believe, is the most awesome visual of patience and waiting on God. Adam is asleep and God is making his match. Relationally, of course, there is a mutual waiting because none of us are in that exact situation Adam found himself in but I have found many couples end up in destructive relationships because they rushed into something instead of waiting on God. He is working on something, even when we're unaware!

Then we see Adam do something that men have been doing for many centuries from the time they are toddlers! Marking their territory. I mean there isn't any competition around, yet Adam is still making sure all the animals, and whoever else might have any smart ideas, that Eve is taken. This woman is now mine, he basically says! This is the first status update in the history of humankind! A lot of people who are old school like me believe that men have lost the ability to pursue women and be clear about their intentions. Now I know not everyone is wired the same and there are women that will say this sounds prehistoric, but God creates a scenario here that is His design. Adam is very clear about how he feels as soon as he feels his feelings, if you know what I mean. He's blown away by her completely and makes a statement about who this woman is to him. Now guys, if you're reading this we gotta be better than stringing girls along and constantly postponing the DTR talk in the hopes of waiting for something better. I find that in most cases, or at least when I was young and dumb, there was a hesitation to be content and grateful that there was a woman in my life willing to pursue Jesus and a future together. Most young men are with someone but are also fetty wapping (using one eye) other potential options that lie outside of their current relationship. Women, if you're honest with each other, you also don't object to this behavior or else a reality show about a guy who is doing this with thirty odd women wouldn't be one of the highest rated shows in its nine hundredth season. See, Adam didn't wait around to see if God was going to create another one of these majestic beings which, to be honest, was a possibility. Eve was more than enough for him—she was better than enough.

I love that in his acknowledgement of this beauty he saw before him that Adam didn't stop doing what he was created to do. His job was literally to name things and as soon as he was done with stating his claim on Eve, he continued to serve God in the way he was created to. I always tell the young couples that I lead that a good way to see if the person you're with is good for you is to ask yourself this question: do they allow me to continue serving God with the same intensity I had before I met them? Or do they pull me away from Him? Ladies, listen to me here, you were created with a purpose by God and so were you dudes. So when we stop functioning in our purpose and doing what we're meant to be doing, we find that the ripple effects of that are not good and can cause havoc in our lives. Our relationships flourish the more we continue our pursuit of serving God rather than slowing that down.

This is a very important thing to understand before you dive into a relationship, and to be honest you probably want to guard this the most. Declaring your priority to serve God right at the beginning weeds out the knock-offs and keeps that space in your life reserved for the ones designed by God to enter it. There may be people you find yourself getting to know in a romantic way but it doesn't end up in marriage and that isn't a bad thing if you honor God in that relationship. So Adam continues to serve God and this leads into the purpose for marriage. It isn't about sex, attraction, kids, or building an empire. If you want that you can find your satisfaction by playing Settlers of Catan. No, a marriage is made for more than that—it is made to reflect the awesome wonder of our God!

COVENANT NOT CONTRACT

After the wedding (or in this case, Adam's vows), God sets in motion the way this works best. We find that in Genesis 2:24 but we also see it in a broader context in another passage, Ephesians 5:21-33.

21 Submit to one another out of reverence for Christ.

22 Wives, submit yourselves to your own husbands as you do to the Lord. 23 For the husband is the head of the wife as Christ is the head of the church, his body, of which he is the Savior. 24 Now as the church submits to

Christ, so also wives should submit to their husbands in everything.

25 Husbands, love your wives, just as Christ loved the church and gave himself up for her 26 to make her holy, cleansing her by the washing with water through the word, 27 and to present her to himself as a radiant church, without stain or wrinkle or any other blemish, but holy and blameless. 28 In this same way, husbands ought to love their wives as their own bodies. He who loves his wife loves himself. 29 After all, no one ever hated their own body, but they feed and care for their body, just as Christ does the church— 30 for we are members of his body. 31 "For this reason a man will leave his father and mother and be united to his wife, and the two will become one flesh." 32 This is a profound mystery—but I am talking about Christ and the church. 33 However, each one of you also must love his wife as he loves himself, and the wife must respect her husband.

In this passage we see what a biblical marriage looks like. We get to peek beyond the hype and see the hope. We also see its greater purpose and where it is meant to function—in a covenant.

God starts with the instruction that the husband will leave his father and mother and be joined to his wife. This means no more mama's boy or daddy's little girl. In my culture, I found this to be true—where there is a failure to realize that you are now part of a new team there are devastating repercussions. The door to the meddling of the family that is meant to be left behind shouldn't be left open because it so often causes strife in the marriage. Moms, I know it is difficult to let go of your little boy, but he's a man now with a woman he has chosen to be with. Let them grow together, let them work out what they need to work out as a couple. I speak to the moms because that was my take away after watching *Crazy Rich Asians*. Even as I write this I have a hunch that tells me it's not just in my culture where this happens but true across many cultures. So the first instruction to this foundational marital thing called a covenant is a resounding message to the man and woman— this is now your closest family, your next of kin. This is now the Simmons to your Embiid, the Cagney to your Lacey, The Kobe to your Shaq, The Chic-Fil-A sauce to your nuggets.

YOU ARE A TEAM. YOU ARE ONE. THIS IS A COVENANT!

What is marriage ultimately *for*? We live in a culture that wants the design while having nothing to do with the designer, God. The problem is when you copy the design and reject the designer it doesn't quite work out right. Marriage is a covenant made by two people brought together by Jesus and it shouldn't be easy to break. The constant picture painted in both the passages we've seen so far is this idea of the two becoming one flesh. This imagery should resonate with every person who has ever stubbed their toe or anyone who has ever had an ingrown nail. If you think that is painful, think about how painful it must be to cut yourself in half. Okay, I don't even have to go that far. Think about how hard it must be to lose even just your pinky. We are quite attached to our bodies, aren't we? And now, the two have become one 'flesh', one body! A covenant between a husband and wife should be the most difficult thing to break unless it is threatening your life.

About a year ago I discovered that one of the drugs I take for my transplanted kidney was causing a spike in my A1C count which measures my blood sugar. So I was slowly getting diabetes. Now my doctor told me there was a way to avoid this from getting worse without stopping the much-needed drug. She told me that I would have to mostly quit sugar and lose weight. She also told me that the effects of diabetes can be terrible including possible amputations if I didn't put in the work. Listen, the moment I heard about amputation, I was ready to quit sugar on the spot! It has now been a few years of avoiding sugar in all my drinks, lowering my carb intake and losing weight. Here is the point I'm making: I love sugary things! But when it was pressed against losing a part of me, it wasn't even a question. To avoid possible amputation I said goodbye to something that I thought I couldn't live without. I quit sugar! I know there are many that don't quit sugar when they hear this and they end up losing legs and limbs. They just choose to roll the dice and believe that it will never have to come to amputation—but it does in the end. In our marriages there has to be a revelation of "one flesh" that helps us prioritize removing everything that could cause us to lose part of our flesh. The only time doctors consider amputation is when it is life threatening and we too should take this covenant thing so seriously that the only time we consider a marital amputation (divorce) is when it is also life threatening.

Here is where it gets real tricky: how do we keep a covenant in a world that is full of contracts? There is no other agreement on this earth besides the one we have with God that looks like marriage does. Everything else is contractual and when one member of the contract fails to uphold their end, we cancel. We feel justified in our cancellation the moment we are not satisfied, the moment we don't get any joy from it.

There is a show on Netflix called, *Tidying up with Marie Kondo*. I watched one episode and (full disclosure) I literally only ever watched one episode and my heart was set on cleaning my whole house. So I started where I knew I had the most junk—my closet. The whole idea is obviously tidying up your life by getting rid of excess and the way Marie Kondo gets there is by telling you to pick up each item of clothing and asking yourself: does this spark joy? If it doesn't spark joy you put it in the discard pile. Wait, if it doesn't spark joy she asks you to thank the piece of clothing before putting it away—weird flex, but okay.

Now that's not how I personally decided on what I threw away. Instead I asked, "Does this top button close or can I lift my hands in worship without people seeing my underwear?" Here is the thing. She says if it doesn't spark joy then thank it and throw it away. Thank you, next! your wardrobe is Marie Kondo's vibe. I don't have a covenant with my pants so I can donate them to someone. But if I told you how many times I have seen people say this about their marriages you would think I'm making it up. The reason you walk away from a covenant is not the same as why you discard clothing. There are times I knew when I was waiting at the end of that isle for my bride that she would not spark joy in me. I knew that there may be days, weeks, months where that there may be no joy, but I was still saying "I do". Covenant, not contract!

I can't discard my flesh because it doesn't spark joy in me anymore and, believe me, there are many parts of me that don't look the way they used to ten years ago (stay tuned for chapter 4). I don't just cut them off, though! If my belly isn't sparking joy in me anymore I don't cut it off but rather I work it out. We don't liposuction our marriages, we P90X it! We are in a covenant! Part of loving her is submitting to Christ in keeping that covenant. My marriage is more than how I feel that day, that week, that month, or that year. If marriage is a reflection of Christ and His bride and I know that He's not leaving her then I shouldn't be easily swayed to do leave mine too.

Now in Ephesians 5 we see that the Bible speaks of roles in this relationship and how these roles lead to an even greater understanding of the mystery of this union. It starts in verse 21.

21 Submit to one another out of reverence for Christ.

22 Wives, submit yourselves to your own husbands as you do to the Lord.

There are two verses I know for sure I can't put on a coffee cup and give my wife without one of us ending up on an episode of Dateline. The one we just read. The other is 1 Corinthians 7:5 (look it up).

With all kidding aside I know this to be true because Ephesians 5:21,22 are loaded verses. As I write this I realize I am about to type across a minefield. My words could be reinforcing years of bigotry and oppression, giving a controlling husband the ammunition to continue to dictate each and every move their wife makes. Over the years this passage has been distorted to mean something it completely does not, and therefore I proceed with a desperate leaning in to what the Holy Spirit is asking me to pen in this moment.

When I was twelve-years-old I got home from school one day and my mom was gone. Now I have to say this—even writing this down years later is difficult because of the weight of it but it is something I must share. I love my parents with all my heart. My dad is not the same guy he was when I was twelve and to some degree my parents have reconciled even though they have been divorced for a long time now. That day, though—that day was one of the hardest, most confusing days of my life. My mom had packed her bags and left my dad. Even though I had sorrow in my heart because my mother was not there that night, a part of me was relieved that my mom was never going to have to endure another day in our home again. I remember, as my dad drove out that evening, he handed my brother and I a fifty dollar bill almost as a way of comforting us in the only way he knew in that moment. My brother and I both looked at each other knowing that life was going to look very different from that point on. As the car faded in the distance I knew my dad had his own heart and sadness to deal with in the only way he knew how.

The next day my mom called us and told us what happened and my brothers and I pretty much spent most of our teenage years living in our new normal—back and forth, having different sets of clothes, different friends and family in two different places. My mom had endured much over the years and I knew for her this decision was not a failure to "spark joy" but more a life-saving one. I will stop there because I know her story is hers to tell but as a child I couldn't deny that she absolutely did the right thing.

We have all, to some degree, seen this passage in Ephesians abused in one way, shape or form but it shouldn't take away from God's plan and design for marriage. The day my mom left has always affected the way I viewed this passage until I read the whole thing and finally took the time to understand what Paul is saying and to whom he is saying it to. The enemy will distort every good thing God has created. In the hands of the enemy, sex becomes porn, wine becomes drunkenness, food becomes gluttony, submission becomes oppression. I am so encouraged by the fact that Ephesus looks much like the world we are in today and that this letter to the church there was written to a church that was smack dab in the middle of a progressive and religiously inclusive society that needed truth spoken to it, especially in the subject of relationships. I am also grateful that as I studied this, I read the whole thing and placed the words in context to finally understand what is being said. In fact I started reading in verse 21.

21 Submit to one another out of reverence for Christ.

There is a *mutual submission*—one hundred percent given from each person as a way of honoring Christ. There is Jesus at the center of it all and both husband and wife are submitting to Him. Ladies, I want you to know this. I want any female that picks up this book to understand that this is the foundation to the rest of this chapter. There are women all over the world being asked to endure abuse after abuse because "it's what God wants". I am calling bull on that and telling you that God isn't calling someone to live in terror just because they are in a covenant with someone. God is also asking something of that man in that covenant and every situation has to be carefully and individually assessed, but I don't have to be a theologian to know that there is no way God wants a woman to be screaming for her life or be constantly belittled—to keep placing themselves in the line of fire.

If there is a man doing this to a woman but also claiming to be a follower of Christ then they do not know Christ because Jesus would never lead someone to darkness. Verse 22, which calls women to submit to their own husbands, comes out of a mutual submission to Christ, and it is sandwiched by that notion and imagery of a husband who is continually laying down his life for his wife. That is where submission comes from. It comes from seeing a love that is continuously sacrificing for the other and that is leading and wooing her to Jesus. Christ is the head of the home and in all that Christ is saying this—girl, love this guy by letting him lead you in a sacrificial way and dude, love this woman by laying down your life in the way that I have done for you. Not conditional, not based on what the other does. The verse doesn't ask guys to make sure their wives are submitting, it just says lay down your life and trust Jesus to change the hearts involved. Women, it also doesn't say submit to all men, it says submit to your own husbands. This beautiful endless picture of mutual submission to Christ, to each other, and a continuous laying down of one's life for the other, is the beautiful picture of marriage that we all long to see in our own lives.

This is the way marriage works best. This is the way our lives work best. I try to remember this question whenever I feel like my way is better than God's way: "Rob, how far has your way taken you, and how far has God's way taken you?" If you're still reading this and you're saying to yourself, "Why am I still reading this?" well this is why, my friend. Dating is necessary in our world today to get to marriage. Listen it's not essential but it is necessary in our culture. Marriage and this ultimate glorification of who Christ is should be the ultimate goal of all dating. Remember whether it leads to marriage at the end of the day is not failure as long as what is pure and glorifying to God was present.

THE HYPE

There is a hype around dating culture that exists today and to be honest most of it is self-centered and doesn't point to God, even in Christian circles. I am a young adult pastor writing parts of this chapter on Valentines Day and I can't help but see the hype that surrounds me. Young single guys and girls feel like they aren't good enough. Negative thoughts are reinforced by a world that says you aren't anything unless you've got somebody. Maybe it's parents putting on pressure as they bring out their biological alarm clocks to remind their kids to get on with it. Or it could even be the church with our endless pleas for single people to volunteer because they have no real purpose, right? No matter who you are, you would have to be blind not to see the hype.

But as I keep reiterating, hype has a shelf life. When hype is gone it is gone for good. I don't know what will come in the coming years but since we couldn't see dating apps coming we probably can't see the next thing around the corner either. The statistics on how dating has morphed into nothing other than a one-night stand is overwhelming. We may be dismissing people with a mere swipe but God doesn't roll like that. God is constantly calling us to be more like Him, more sensitive to His beautiful plan for relationships and marriage. God is not ghosting us and leaving us with no hope. If we lean on Him we don't have to idly watch the hype wash away and then wait to count the casualties. He says you must be different. He says, you must point others to better, and better is Me.

THE HOPE

It's obvious that we are created for relationships with one another and that God has wired us with a great desire to find that person we can do this thing called life with. The hope of what we long for in relationships can be found in the answers to these questions: why do relationships exist? And why do I want to be in one?

We know that relationships exist to bring glory to God. We see that even in the Ephesians passage we've been looking at that Paul pauses and says, "Hey, I'm not talking about relationships here but rather I'm talking about Jesus and the Church!" Check it out:

32 This is a profound mystery—but I am talking about Christ and the church. 33 However, each one of you also must love his wife as he loves himself, and the wife must respect her husband.

It is as though Paul has taken the church in Ephesus through this whole deal on marriage just to get to go, "You know what? I'm not even talking about marriage, but rather I'm talking about Jesus and the Church!" He makes it clear that this is where the hope of marriage lies and therefore here also lies the hope in dating. Note that I am not saying the wedding. This truth we find in the book of

Ephesians is talking about our for ever commitment in marriage. The hope is marriage should reflect Jesus to those who are watching.

I have to say this for the person reading this who may be saying, "Rob, it's over for me. I messed up so bad I could never get married." Or the person saying, "I'm already divorced and I'm now a single mom or single dad." There may even be people saying, "Rob, I am not married to someone who believes in Jesus so we don't even have a shot at mutual submission." I think of those scenarios as I think of people I lead or even loved ones close to me. You may feel discarded like the clothes in that show *Tidying Up*, but the beauty of what marriage reflects is also one of a savior who never gave up on us and came to save us in our state. He loved us as He found us! I would say that the cross is a picture of Jesus metaphorically driving to every donation center and picking us up as we are. As we were put away for no longer sparking joy in someone else He looked at us and said, "You spark joy in *me*!" Yes, you spark joy in Jesus! So much joy that He was willing to give up His life and suffer much pain to get you. There was no price God the Father was unwilling to pay to win you back. So if He loves us that much, how much more would He be willing to pour grace where the ideal is lacking in your life?

I remember soon after my parents separated I befriended a guy in my high school and God used his parents to pour grace on my life and show me what a godly marriage looked like. I remember when I would spend weekends at his house I would wonder how a husband and wife could live so peacefully and respect one another so much; how a dad would choose to be with his family on the weekend instead of at a bar with his friends. How they did things as a family at all times! They played such an integral role in my life that his dad actually gave a speech at my wedding and it was beautiful!

In everything we do we have to always be aware of the God-aspect of it or else we will always give into the hype and miss the hope.

4

SELF IMAGE

So I think I'm fat!

Yeah I said the "F" word. Fat! Fat happens, I know, and it has most definitely happened to me.

Now I don't mean obese, or that my body parts are bulging out of my skinny jeans. I just mean that I'm in the state of not being skinny, fit, or physically attractive. So as I was saying, I think I'm fat, and by now I know you're tempted to look at the perfectly photoshopped version of me that is on the back of this book. Don't! I will make sure to get the thinnest most polished version of myself before this gets printed.

Real talk and kidding aside, it really is what I think of myself, and I know there are many people in my circle of friends who would say that this is ridiculous thinking on my part. Some, though, would agree with my now five-year-old, brutally honest, no-filter-having daughter who just told me this afternoon as I took my shirt off to swim—"Dad, you have a poppy belly". Poppy belly for those of you who don't understand is five-year-old for... I guess... Um, what's the word for it again?... FAT!

Now since this is in this book it means one of two things: my wife read this and said, "I think this is something everyone should read so, go ahead, put it in the book," or I published this without her knowledge and as a result I've been missing for as long as this book has been out. This is a sensitive topic. I know I have to prayerfully navigate this as with every chapter in this book, but I especially need to do this because I haven't always thought this way about myself. Mainly because I was always the skinny kid that wanted to have more meat on his bones. Unfortunately more recently, thanks to all the American indigenous food I've had over the years, I got more meat on my stomach and my bones are still pretty bare!

As much as it may seem that I'm comfortable talking about this, I have to confess that I know I am diving into territory that has affected many people for much of their lives. I have to think what happens when throwing Psalm 139 at your struggle doesn't get rid of it? I know that this affects way more people than we think because not liking how we look can be an extremely painful internal struggle. Many never share in this struggle because they should be "grateful" they can fit into a size ten and should let the struggle belong to those who "really" struggle. Another issue is that I am a dude... and dudes do not talk about body image. I mean, why would we struggle with body image or how we look? But listen ladies, it's not just you.

We sometimes wish we had a fashion accessory we could just put in front of our bellies. We also work the angles on our selfies to make us look slimmer and I can't remember the last time I didn't hold my breath for a picture! I've done entire church announcement videos without breathing out once! We all don't look like Liam Hemsworth, or is his name Chris? I'm not sure. To be extra safe let's just talk about Mr. Chocolate Perfect Idris Elba and how we are being exposed, through social media, to a standard that most of us can't attain. So as a guy I can say, ladies it's not just a lady struggle anymore than porn is a guy struggle!

Even though I'm struggling with my self-image, I still haven't been in the place where I've dreamed that one day I would turn on my phone, open Instagram and see a dude with a belly like mine in a speedo and Oprah sharing their post with the caption, "the man of our dreams". So I feel like I am on the outside of a struggle that is so crippling to many. I have seen it lead to a self-hatred so intense that people have taken their own lives over it. I have seen incessant bullying lead others into isolation and many have never enjoyed a day at the beach or a public swimming pool because of it. Even though I pointed out that this is also a guy struggle, I absolutely have to tread carefully because this doesn't affect as many men in the same way it affects women due to the misogynistic nature of our culture that has sexually objectified women for centuries, indoctrinating all of us to think of beauty as one thing and one thing only... a size zero, unrealistic blonde with blue eyes that we buy for our kids to play with from day one. Are we still really living in an age where this is a thing? Lately I have seen movements that have started to balance the playing field a little; movements where women of all sizes are encouraged to embrace the beauty of their bodies. I am generally a critical thinker so I thought about my observation of this culture over the last few years and the following is what I came up with.

BODY POSITIVITY

It seemed like the world was always going to be a place where the only acceptable size would be a size zero. Regardless of how many times Sir Mix-a-Lot's "Baby Got Back" played on the airwaves in the 90's, the majority culture was still very much in love with small itty bitty backs! That was until mainstream pop music and culture became the one in which Sir Mix-a-Lot was from. I honestly believe that the body positivity movement is kinda birthed in a mix of the rise of hip-hop culture being mainstream, social media, and Kim Kardashian's rise to fame. Yes you read right, Kim K! If the most beautiful woman around according to "mainstream media" isn't a size zero and is the object of much of the male attention, it changes things.

With this change, it meant that the 90's version of beauty like Kate Moss and Madonna had to get in the gym and get their squat game on! I am pretty sure that Malcom Gladwell's research on this topic will be richer than my personal observations but I will continue. So factor in this change and then factor in something we may not want to come to terms with but is the truth... The rise of yoga pants and leggings meant that actually having a figure was a thing worthy of being celebrated. Excuse my very accurate observation here but we are now living in Sir Mix-a-Lot's world! Add a sprinkling of social media mob public justice leading to the rise in bullies being publicly shamed and excommunicated from society and voila! There you have it ladies and gents, the perfect swell for a movement that accepts bodies of all different shapes and sizes!

Now it isn't all positive though. See, that movement can be pretty exclusive and sexually revealing. The need wasn't just for my body type to be accepted but to also be *acknowledged as sexy*. Now sexy and comfortable are two different things. I want my wife to think I'm sexy but I don't necessarily want to be sexy to everyone else. As my very good-looking friend who shall remain unnamed used to tell me, "You don't want that kind of vibe." See, his rationale was everywhere he goes, girls just want to be with him because of how he looks and nothing else. Guys always assume he's a jerk and want nothing to do with him. I believe him because hanging out with him changes how often waitresses come to our table (too much) and it changes the environment completely wherever we go. It actually isn't cool.

So when the aim is sexy it leads to sensuality. We've all been exposed to what sensuality looks like so let's not kid ourselves. No one has to spell it out for you. My point being, with the rise of a good movement, the pendulum swung all the way to the other side and we were exposed to more women being sexually objectified in the name of body positivity. See, all you have to do is follow the hashtag #bodypositive and find that it's mainly women, with the majority showing you how comfortable they are with exposing their sexuality in the name of positivity. My point in the early parts of this chapter is the reason why this movement doesn't work for men is because it has a sexual objectification angle to it that we may not really want to face head-on right now. If you have never felt ashamed of your body, how would you even start to talk about what people should or shouldn't do with their freedom? I mean, what do I really know about this, as a guy? But I do know that we all have to search for the deeper meaning of our longing to be accepted, because any good thing can quickly turn into a bad thing. It just needs the wrong people to grab a hold of it and down the drain we go.

So Rob, hope over hype. Where is the hope, bro? Look, I'm a pastor and we're a few paragraphs in and I haven't even brought up God yet because I want to be clear that my approach to this subject of image is something I am not just trying to whack over the head with a passage of scripture or smother in a rewritten version of my favorite Christian blog post. This is real. Also, this chapter might be my book of Esther... If you know, you know. (Okay you probably don't know but the book of Esther is the only book in the Bible where God gets *zero* mentions.)

I realize there is no magic bullet to answer the question

we have about self love and what the right dose of confidence is before it becomes sensuality. I do think that often being told you are beautiful doesn't hurt, right? So being the dad of two amazing girls I tell them as often as I can that they are beautiful. I know one day just me saying that might not be enough so I hope to build a big ministry so that there will always be young men trying to suck up to me so they will treat my daughters like gold! Real strategy revealed there. All joking aside, I remind them when they feel like they aren't enough or their hair isn't pretty enough that all of who they are is precious and what they may think are flaws are the things that make them special to me. I wish I did this more for my wife so that she wouldn't doubt that I think she is gorgeous! But I am flawed and dumb and don't do it enough.

Before my recent struggle with my body, which I could change if I just changed my eating habits, worked out, and drank more water (it's never that easy), I had another big image issue. What? You must be thinking, dude, you may need to read your own book and get some help. It's okay to think that, it may be the reason why I felt so strongly that I should write a chapter on image.

TOOTH GAP

I have this gap between my two front teeth. You can't miss it and if you meet me you'll remember it. I have been that way all my life and when I was younger girls let me know about it, teachers described me to others by pointing it out, and (of course) some dumb girl told me that she didn't like my smile and that's why I would never be an option. I mean she didn't say it to me directly, I just heard her say the most important thing to her was teeth and I knew I was out of the running! So for years I was cool with it, as in, I never ever thought about changing it. I always felt secure in who I was in the other areas of my life and hey, I'm funny, so you know a sense of humor can win people even when you think you lack in other areas. I mean someone obviously liked me the way I was... they married me!

But recently I noticed that the more I stood in front of people, the more I began to lose confidence in smiling without putting my hand in front of my mouth or not smiling at all. I didn't want to be the gap-tooth guy. So now I'm compounding more and more insecurity into this chapter. I mean people who have heard me say this remind me that Michael Strahan has a gap too! I always think to myself, did they just say that I should be fine with my flaw because a millionaire, Super Bowl champion, Hall of Fame inductee, who is dating a supermodel and has an incredibly successful television career has one too? Really? I mean I get what they're saying but it's very logical. We live with our insecurities and we have them all day, every day: every interaction, every moment we're in front of a mirror, every time we see an ad with someone wearing something we could never pull off. These thoughts can dominate our thought life and steal our joy at every given opportunity. So how do we defeat this beast, while finding the right balance between health, joy, and a God-honoring posture, all at the same time? When you find that out, contact me because I'm dying to know!

I'll be even more vulnerable and share how I got to the root of my insecurity in order to snap the crap thoughts right at the root and not just clip the bad fruit. I got braces! No, not really... I got spiritual braces, which involves digging right into the root of my issues.

YOUR MOTHER

"I'm your mother and if I don't tell you no one will love you enough to tell you." That line always followed a comment from my mother about how we looked when we were kids. I remember experiencing most of this by watching my older brother's reaction. He had this laugh that exposed a lot of his gums. He was just a joyful guy, quirky and big for his age. He was pretty funny to look at when he laughed. He also couldn't dance, wasn't all that funny (now he is) but he had this going for him... he was always the smartest guy in the room and ridiculously athletic. All those traits are impossible to find in one person but for all his positives he had that weird-looking smile. Now I didn't think it was weird at all, it was my brother's smile, but if he really had a good laugh, his lip would flip over a bit. I loved that because as his personal jester it meant I had done my job. I like making people laugh, it literally brings me joy, so I was always trying to do it. The problem is, if you have a mix of a bad-looking laugh and a little brother that constantly makes you laugh around someone who is constantly telling you that your laugh is ugly then that can be a pretty damaging thing.

Thankfully, my older brother has a thick skin and he also corrected his laugh. Unfortunately for me, a seven on the enneagram and an ENFJ, which means I'm the feeler of all feelers, I never wanted my mother saying that said to me in that tone... like never ever. The funny thing is, my mom and I share a physical feature in common: we both have the gap. The official term for it is *diastema* and it is a dominant gene, meaning this thing is as hereditary as hereditary can be! I grew up watching my mom navigate the years I'm navigating right now, so maybe she was cool with it all her life and then one season, like the one I'm having now, she became conscious of it and started to cover her mouth a bit when she laughed around new people. I noticed that she didn't like her teeth and she may have even said it which made me ever more conscious of it. Now factor in a mean kid here and there, a girl rejecting you, years of watching my smile-conscious mom cover her flaw, the same one I have, and the image-conscious seed was sown.

I had to deal with my mommy issues concerning my teeth. It wasn't easy but I had to really think about why I felt the way I did about myself. We can usually be cool with one thing being a little off but when you compound our flaws it's too much for our neocortex to deal with. The neocortex is part of the cerebral cortex and it is involved in higher functions such as sensory perception, generation of motor commands, spatial reasoning, conscious thought—and in humans, language. When meeting someone new, conscious thought can't be thinking about a book or a handbag to put in front of your belly as well as a hand to cover your mouth at the same time. We literally can only handle one insecurity at a time before it becomes impossible to even leave our house.

So after getting to the root as a follower of Christ, my heart should go to the one I have the greatest relationship with. This is when Jesus becomes a central piece to the image puzzle. Who we are has to be rooted in *whose* we are and if that is out of sync we can't honestly defeat the demons that plague us and try to own the space of worship that is meant to be occupied by God. We must ask: what does God think about how I look? And is it important that I fix it?

WHY IMAGE MATTERS

What do you see when you look in the mirror? Do you look at that image and love it? See, what we look like matters and it is a fact that men and women respond to their reflection differently. Roughly eight out of ten women will be dissatisfied with their reflection, yet men in general will be either pleased or indifferent to the image they see. The main reason why men and women react differently is largely due to the fact that the media judges women more and has established a very rigid standard for what beauty is. Image matters and it matters not just because media throws out a bunch of lies about our looks but because we are with ourselves twenty-four hours a day and if you don't like who you're with all the time it can be daunting.

There is a bigger reason why image matters though... It matters because of these words in the first chapter of Genesis.

26 Then God said, "Let us make mankind in our image, in our likeness, so that they may rule over the fish in the sea and the birds in the sky, over the livestock and all the wild animals, and over all the creatures that move along the ground."

27 So God created mankind in his own image, in the image of God he created them; male and female he created them.

God says, "let us make man in our likeness and our image." I love that those are the exact words used because this is big in understanding a key word that is found at the core of our image woes. This word is *value*. These two verses in the Bible make it clear to all of us right from the start that we are made in the image of God. When we look at each other we get to see what God looks like.

Let me not get ahead of myself though—let's talk about image and likeness.

THE ICONIC IMAGE

In February 1988, Nike released the iconic Nike Air Jordan III. This shoe was the first shoe designed by the man who would become the "Jordan whisperer," Tinker Hatfield. The reason why this shoe is so iconic to all sneakerheads out there is because this is the first Jordan sneaker to feature the iconic Jumpman logo. This image of Michael Jordan jumping with a ball at the end of an outstretched arm is a thing of beauty. As a kid growing up in Africa, this image is one that I dreamt of seeing over and over again whenever someone would come back from the USA. Now if you are a Gen-xer like me you will know the feels you got when you put your feet inside your first (possibly only) pair of Jordans. I can't tell you what it was about this image on the tongue of a pair of shoes that drove people crazy, but it did. To this day it's still a thing that jogs something in me when I see the new retro releases online.

Here is the wild thing about that logo. it was licensed for $150 by Peter Moore, the designer of the first two Jordan releases. It generates $3 billion in revenue annually! I mean slap this logo on something and the value of that article of clothing goes way up! The Jordan brand is a powerhouse and is arguably the most famous athletic brand of all time. Jordan is the only Nike product that can sell without a Nike Swoosh in sight. See, whether it is a Bred (black and red) pair of Jordan 1's or it's the all-white History of Flight Jordan 13's, as long as Michael Jordan's image and likeness is on them they have value and someone somewhere is bound to love them!

Now there is more. Not to blow your mind here, but there is a guy named Virgil... Virgil Abloh. He is a high fashion designer out of Chicago who was given a project by Nike to recreate some of the most iconic Jordan sneakers. When Virgil designs a pair of Jordan sneakers their value, due to the low supply, high demand and unique appearance, reaches astronomical levels! A pair of Virgil Abloh designed Jordans are valued as high as $4,400 a pair! You might be thinking, "$4,400 for a pair of Nikes? Are you kidding?" If you are, you might be outside of the target market for this book, and I am truly grateful you are still reading. Seriously though, I have just given you a quick lesson on the current sneaker market and the power of branding.

I used this example because we are like these shoes that have been slapped with a logo in the image and likeness of someone iconic and have been designed by the designer of all designers! So when we look at a pair of deconstructed sneakers with a sharpie inscription on the sole that to some may be one of the ugliest things they have ever seen, we have to realize that the value is not based on whether or not we think the product is beautiful, the value is based on what image is on the product and who designed it. We are like the illest Jordans, only our logo is the God logo and our designer is known for making the most beautiful things ever. Think the Victoria Falls, the Grand Canyon, my wife and kids, the galaxy... I could go on but I'll be driving the word count up unnecessarily. You get what I'm saying here. *You are valuable!*

When we look in the mirror we see what God looks like. Every one of us. I mean I don't even know how to let that sink right to the depths of my soul, in all honesty. God says, "I am going to highlight myself, right click, copy and paste myself multiple times in multiple colors and multiple fonts and font sizes," and out comes you and I. If we believe that we have a Father in Heaven that has made us look like Him, and we have an enemy that can't get to Him because He is God, we have to think that our image struggles affect almost each and every one of us because it is the only way the enemy can even remotely get close to attacking God Himself. The utter darkness in our inability to love how we look is also magnified in the sense that when we say we don't like how we look we are rejecting how God says He looks. We are actively buying into the assault on our Father in Heaven by joining a chorus of millions, maybe billions, that have been deceived into rejecting how their creator looks and designed them.

Now some may say God was only talking about Adam and Eve in Genesis, and they must have been gorgeous specimens of human beings. I mean they ate all organic and vegan, breathed one hundred percent pure oxygen, and there was Fiji water everywhere. Zero percent body fat! Maybe or maybe not. Regardless, we are all their descendants anyway so we all have some trait of our first relatives.

Now that we can see that we are valuable, we can start to remind ourselves of that first and foremost. Look, I know that "God thinks you're beautiful" is not what our hearts want to hear, as well as hearing our moms tell us how good-looking we are. But telling ourselves that we are of great worth is a critical starting point to crushing the lies that try and drown our souls. We have to be able to shout louder than our insecurities because they will shout without any effort at all. While we can't change what attractive means to everyone else, we can change how we see ourselves. Attractive is what attractive is. We all know when we see an incredibly attractive person. We all know when we look good and when we look like it's not our day. We can't trick the world into changing its mind but we can change our own minds and begin to live in the freedom of our worth. Attractiveness is not our goal, freedom is!

THE HYPE

The hype on image is this: If we can just find acceptance from the attractive people, if people think we're sexy, then we'd be happy. If that was true, and I mean if that were really true, there would be no beautiful people that hate the way they look—and there are plenty of those. If that were true there wouldn't be a single person who has graced the cover of a fashion magazine that doesn't struggle with their image or drug use or depression and anxiety in the fashion or film industry. These are the people who are on the covers and are in the commercials that claim to be the blinking neon arrows to happiness. Rather, the reality is this—*whatever you look like, you are beautiful.* Maybe you feel like you need to hit the gym again so that you can fit those Lulu Lemon leggings you've been eyeing, there is nothing wrong with that. Maybe you need braces so that you can have a more confident smile when you meet people. All good. Just know this: fitting the leggings or having the straighter smile isn't going to make you any more than you are now. It may give you a little confidence here and there but it won't get to the root of why you feel the way you feel about yourself.

THE HOPE

We have to deal with the root of this issue. The root of all our messes is we have an enemy that has a plan to defile everything good God has made. The enemy is the one that constantly whispers to you that you are not worth anything when heaven constantly echoes that you are to die for!

> But God demonstrates his own love for us in this: While we were still sinners, Christ died for us. (Romans 5:8)

That verse says that you were worth it *all* to him. I have watched my fair share of romance and have read all the fairytales and there is always this theme of a damsel in distress (usually a princess) and a prince who is willing to prove his love by risking it all to save her. God showed His love for you and I—he showed how much He values those that bear His image by sending His most precious, sinless, pure Son, Jesus to reclaim us. To reclaim all of us *as we are*!

While we were yet sinners, while we had the gap tooth, while we had the frizzy hair, the cellulite, eczema, the baby pooch, the crooked finger and nose, the hairy arms, the unibrow... He died for all that before the botox, before the laser hair removal, before the Atkins, Weight Watchers, $9 trillion exercise bike, Photoshop and Instagram filters! The hope is we were valuable before we felt it. You may not feel like you have the perfect body but in the every day, each and every one of us make up God's perfect body.

MONEY

So I have a message for you. You're a pretty selfish person.

The reason I know this to be a fact is because you don't give as much as you can and you put yourself first way more than you should.

Now I know, I know, you're saying what I usually tell myself. I give as much as I can, Rob. I do my part. Whatever "my part" means. Now unless you have already admitted that you're selfish (which means you can skip the next few lines) I want us to get this out of the way so that the main passage in this chapter makes sense.

The best compass of where we're at with God is our bank account. That is our treasure and what we do with our treasure determines what we treasure. Like Jay-Z is famously known for saying in his 2009 American Music Awards (AMA) acceptance speech, "Men lie, women lie, numbers don't." Touché Mr Carter, touché. Numbers don't lie (now my hip's another story) and my bank account numbers reveal how much I love me some Rob Chifokoyo.

I believe this is the reason Jesus spoke about money more than any other subject. Money is important and it has the ability to rule over us if we don't pay careful attention to its role in our life. Now I'm by no means rich but I do live in a place where the median income is much closer to $100k per year, yet I come from a city in Zimbabwe where the average income is $3,300 per year. So to the people in my community I'm at the lower end of the income scale, but to the people from my hometown in Harare, Zimbabwe, I'm a baller!

I say that to help set the foundation for our understanding of what rich really is. Wealth is a subjective thing and how rich I am is usually determined by who I'm comparing myself to. If I'm comparing my laminate kitchen countertops to the granite and marble my neighbor's have, then no, I'm not rich; but if I'm comparing the fact that I actually have running water in my kitchen as opposed to some of my relatives who haven't seen that in years, then that's another story.

THE RICH YOUNG RULER

Arguably, my favorite passage about Jesus and money is the story of the rich young ruler. There are so many stories of people who have interactions with Jesus that I can dismiss at face value because I don't fit the profile. With this particular story though, I don't quite have that luxury. I can't dismiss myself from it because it speaks of almost everything that I have felt, said and asked Jesus at one point or another. It stings because of how close to home it hits, but it has revealed so much of me to myself and more of my dependence on stuff rather than God. So let's take a look at how it unfolds.

> As Jesus started on his way, a man ran up to him and fell on his knees before him. "Good teacher," he asked, "what must I do to inherit eternal life?"
>
> 18 "Why do you call me good?" Jesus answered. "No one is good—except God alone. 19 You know the commandments: 'You shall not murder, you shall not commit adultery, you shall not steal, you shall not give false testimony, you shall not defraud, honor your father and mother.
>
> 20 "Teacher," he declared, "all these I have kept since I was a boy."
>
> 21 Jesus looked at him and loved him. "One thing you lack," he said. "Go, sell everything you have and give to the poor, and you will have treasure in heaven. Then come, follow me."
>
> 22 At this the man's face fell. He went away sad, because he had great wealth. (Mark 10:17-22)

I remember the day I smoked my first cigarette. My dad used to smoke a cigarette in the morning before taking us to school. In the lead up to smoking for the first time, I watched his movements carefully each morning like a bank robber scopes a bank. I was patiently waiting for the perfect opportunity to grab a puff of this thing that had all the elements a kid would want (or at least that's what I thought). I must have been about seven-years-old at the time and you can imagine why smoking would be appealing to a kid my age. I mean what wasn't appealing? You had the act of striking a match, then fire, the act of making smoke come out of your mouth, and the fact that you're not allowed to do it. All the other things that the grown-ups had that we were prohibited like Coca-Cola and chocolates were awesome, so this must be too, right?

One morning he puffed away as he usually did but this time I had calculated when I could pounce and grab the cigarette as he threw it away. When my moment came I quickly grabbed it and took a drag! And what followed was the worst feeling my mouth, chest, throat and tongue ever felt. It was the grossest thing ever! I immediately threw it away, coughed profusely, and ran to the car to go to school. From that point on, I knew that smoking was one of the worst things I could ever do. But I also began carrying the burden of the heaviest secret my little heart had ever harbored. The chest pain I was feeling at the time and the difficulty I had breathing could not be revealed to anyone due to the fear of the potential exposure of my disobedience. Even though no one would ever find out, I had to live with the consequences of the secrecy of my actions. I walked away from that and was still a sweet obedient seven-year-old in everyone's eyes except the only eyes that truly knew that I wasn't... my own. We are often limited in what we see in others because we can't actually see a person in full. We can only see what people allow us to see, but on the flip side Jesus sees all of us. He sees everything. With that in mind think about how this story of the rich young ruler speaks to the unknown parts of this man's life.

Let's look at how the Bible describes this man. He had great wealth. He was young. He obeyed the commandments from his youth. He was handsome. Okay it doesn't say he was handsome in the Bible but come on, let's be real here. I don't know a single pastor on this planet who wouldn't recruit this dude onto some leadership team in a flash. I mean this dude runs after Jesus and he falls at His feet. His desire to chase after Jesus is there; his reverence for His presence is there; and he asks a smarter question than all the disciples had ever asked up until that point. If you're a single lady reading this you know what I'm talking about... this is swipe-right-in-an-instant hubby material, yet Jesus sees beyond the surface.

The Bible says in 1 Samuel 16:6-7

6 When they arrived, Samuel saw Eliab and thought, "Surely the Lord's anointed stands here before the Lord." 7 But the Lord said to Samuel, "Do not consider his appearance or his height, for I have rejected him. The Lord does not look at the things people look at. People look at the outward appearance, but the Lord looks at the heart."

I love this passage because it shows us the perspective

God has of us at all times. Even this super godly prophet looked around and picked Eliab based on what was presented on the outside, yet God was seeing something else. He was looking at the unseen... the heart of the man. We would like to think we are good most of the time, or moderately generous, loving, responsive and kind. Yet when we consider that God sees at all times our hearts, our bank accounts and all the times we haven't said yes to helping someone that we absolutely felt like we should be helping, this should bring us back down to earth. God sees who we really are and oftentimes who we really are is who we are when we think no one is watching. The unseen parts of us reveal so much more of us than our Instagram profiles or our Facebook posts. To be honest those things are probably the least real parts of us, but we live in a world where we have bought the lie that people really are who they present themselves to be on their timelines. But the most revealing parts of us are the parts that will never be displayed for the world to see.

Some of us are guilty of giving wealthy people a pass because the world has somehow drawn this crazy conclusion that if you have money you are worthy of being treated differently. So our temptation is to trust wealthy people even when it's obvious that they are being dishonest or are abusing their power. This happens especially in Zimbabwe. Wealth is attached to blessing and if you're blessed then you must be doing something right, God must be on your side. We want to be friends with people who have accomplished much and be seen with them and in the places in which they roam. We equate wealth and success to mean something more than it truly represents and we all love our rags to riches stories. They're so heartwarming and inspiring, right?

If we were in this story with Jesus we wouldn't respond in the way Jesus responds because we have an already biased view of wealth. If you couple that with the fact that this guy was a good guy then you can understand the disciples' response to Jesus' reception of this man. They ask, "Who then can be saved?" I mean I get it. Jesus, if this good, commandment-keeping rich guy can't be saved, then who can? But all they could see was the exterior—the Instagram profile—but Jesus could see the DM's.

I heard someone say the other day that whatever you rely on in your toughest moment is your god. In our toughest moments, we will run to that unseen god, whatever that may be. We can sing Kumbaya all we want but it is in the moments in life when we are desperate that our hearts are revealed in what we first reach for. Jesus already knew that money was this young man's god and maybe genuinely this guy didn't know that but this is what Jesus does when we come face to face with Him—He shows us the true state of our hearts.

Money being such a private thing means that our spending, giving and saving habits can remain very hidden. It is for this very reason why it can reveal so much about us. We believe that no one will ever see but really, in all honesty, someone does see—Jesus.

THE MONEY MASTER

There is a tribe in Botswana called the San. They are hunter gatherers and thought to be the oldest inhabitants of Southern Africa. The San are arguably best known for their excellent hunting abilities, which were popularized by the great success of the 80's comedy, *The Gods Must Be Crazy*.

Now the San do a fair amount of trapping and one of the coolest things I've seen is how they catch monkeys in the bush. See, monkeys are incredibly elusive and clever, so it takes an equal degree of trickery to catch them. Long ago, the San discovered that monkeys are also very greedy and unwilling to let go of food once they have it. So to catch them, the San dig a small hole in the side of a solid anthill and fill it with food. They make sure that the hole is big enough for a monkey's flat hand to go in, but not big enough for a monkey's clenched hand to get out. They patiently wait for the monkey to find the trail of food and once the monkey finds the motherload in the hole it can't resist. Driven by greed, the monkey slips its hand into the hole and grabs a fistful of food. But now it can't figure out how to get the food out. Even though there is no way to get the food out, the monkey continues to try and pull at it, making it vulnerable to predators and the hunter who set the trap. This is how greedy the monkey is. Even when it sees the hunter coming it still won't loosen its grip on the food and flee to safety. In one swift swoop the hunter grabs the monkey and ties it to a tree and leaves it there.

The monkey's master is its belly and it can't let go of a new found treasure even if it means risking its freedom. We are a lot like the monkey with money—a trap that we fall into time and time again. If you look at this story carefully you will see that there is nothing wrong with the monkey looking for food, in fact it is a very necessary thing for it to do. Just like there is nothing wrong with money. It is only when money is our master that we start to pursue it even at the detriment of our health, freedom, families and close relationships. This is when we become just like the monkey. Some people overwork themselves into a state of bad health in pursuit of money. Some lie, steal and cheat on their taxes when money is their master, and they all risk their freedom. Satan knows that this trap of making money our master is a trap we so easily fall into and, just like the San hunter, he creates a trail for us to follow until we hit the motherload and can't escape due to our own greed. The only way we can live in a healthy relationship with money is when God is supremely our master and money is clearly just a tool.

19 "Do not store up for yourselves treasures on earth, where moths and vermin destroy, and where thieves break in and steal. 20 But store up for yourselves treasures in heaven, where moths and vermin do not destroy, and where thieves do not break in and steal. 21 For where your treasure is, there your heart will be also.

22 "The eye is the lamp of the body. If your eyes are healthy, your whole body will be full of light. 23 But if

your eyes are unhealthy, your whole body will be full of darkness. If then the light within you is darkness, how great is that darkness!

24 "No one can serve two masters. Either you will hate the one and love the other, or you will be devoted to the one and despise the other. You cannot serve both God and money. (Matthew 6:19-24)

I don't know how that hits you, but the last line always hits my heart: "You can't serve both God and money." It is unreal the way our devotion to money can manifest itself. One moment our devotion is entirely to God (or so we think) and then, like the rich young ruler, we have an encounter with Jesus, be it at church or by meeting someone who is a sold-out follower and bam! Our master is revealed. We start to look around and see that we store up earthly treasures and now our lives are built around protecting these treasures and acquiring more and more. We get comfortable with our god of money.

If the way the San catch the monkey is intriguing it is actually what they do with the monkey after that says even more. They tie the monkey to a tree and don't beat it into submission or kill it and eat it, at least not yet. In fact, they do the opposite. They pamper it and feed it all the food it desires. Every few hours they give this monkey all the corn, pods and fruit it could possibly want. They do this so much that the monkey stops trying to break free and starts to become dependent on its new master. Not only that, but the hunter fights off predators and other monkeys trying to steal its food. I can imagine this monkey thinking to itself, "Wow, what a deal! What a great master I have! So loving, full of provision, waiting on me day and night, protecting me while I just sit here and eat." As the monkey gets fat with each meal it forgets that it's tied to a tree and is actually in captivity. And what it doesn't know is the hunter has a big family and he is just fattening it up so that it can feed more of his family when the time comes.

As human beings we're all somewhere on that line in our relationship with money. We're either on the trail, on our way to the hole filled with food, or we're stuck in the hole with our fist trying to get as much as we can even if it risks our freedom. Some of us, yes the ones that look like they've made it, look like they have it all but they've forgotten that they're tied to a tree, that their master is actually setting them up for the slaughter. Now don't get me wrong, I'm not saying money is evil! I am saying what the Bible clearly states: That when it's your master it only leads to evil.

Even though money is necessary and we all need it for one thing or another, we can't be caught up in the madness of chasing it even if it costs us everything. Often when we dedicate our everything to the pursuit of wealth and success we find when we get to the top that there are so many regretful people who sacrificed the things that mattered on the altar of money. This master called money will eventually come to claim what it always intended to claim and that is your soul. The hidden secrets of who your god is will eventually come to light.

PREACHERS AND SNEAKERS

The phenomenon of the Instagram page, Preachers-NSneakers was one such revelation. Pastors who were flexing on their stages and social media platforms were now being exposed as materialistic monsters because of the expensive sneakers they owned. It was a heart check for me and many of my Christian friends who owned a cool pair of Jordan's or, dare I say, Yeezys. For so long as followers of these preachers we had all been given the okay to also be excessive consumers by their braggadocious posts and their subtle but obvious show of wealth. By no means were these guys preaching the prosperity gospel, but they were living a life that consisted of feet that could only be found in $700 sneakers. I mean dude, wear a pair of Vans once in a while!

I believe PreachersNSneakers was the boiling point of the incessant one-upping that happens in the church in America. It wasn't manifesting itself in how many homeless people they were uplifting or communities they were transforming but rather in how many cool sneakers they owned. Look I hate Christian consumerism but I have done my fair share of lining up around a few blocks to hear my favorite worship band. We were the people that got the preachers their sneakers. We paid $160 to worship with them in an arena; we put them on a pedestal of receiving masses amounts of money from book deals, and now we're mad that they bought stuff? I'm just saying I am not without sin and so I shouldn't cast a stone. But with that said it was disappointing hearing these pastors try and explain why they owned these things, why they pursued things that made no sense for a pastor to own or at least flaunt on their platform. The Gucci bags turned brand-side-up at the back... come on! That is flexing! You wanted someone to see that! Here is the deal: the hand was stuck in the anthill and bam! Satan had people questioning everything these guys said, most of which was awesome, life-giving, Christ-centered stuff! But it was now out there to just drop a little seed of doubt and the comments on posts was evidence of that.

Now I don't like that disgruntled ex-church members and skeptics found justification to unfollow Jesus, but this was the enemy's win. It was about preachers who got greedy, projected the wrong master, lacked awareness, and a social media account that exposed them and cast doubt in those who were on the fence.

Eventually what the heart treasures will become evident to all and it's not because we lack the right words, it's because we lack the right heart. Jesus reveals in the heart of the young man where his real desires lie. Yes you do good, yes you have the right words, yes you have the right posture, but my friend you have the wrong savior. See the story of the rich young ruler reveals that if we believe that the one thing that will bring us ultimate happiness is money then it almost doesn't matter what we know, how many times we go to church, or how good we think Jesus is. If our hearts have a different god then we could never truly follow Jesus wholeheartedly. The story of the rich young ruler is more about the consequence of a missed opportunity, and what truly happens when we trust in the wrong master? We miss the greatest thing of all time: following Christ!

THE GOAT

Does the name Stuart Kirk Inman ring a bell in your anyone's head? This highly successful NBA general manager for the Portland Trail Blazers, affectionately called Stu by those in the sporting world, had an amazing career and helped build the 1977 Portland championship team. That alone is an achievement many will never accomplish and it would be fair for you to think that is what Stu is best remembered for, but it isn't. In 1984, Stu was the director of personnel and in charge of scouting and drafting. The draft was loaded with talent and the obvious front runner that year was a young Nigerian by the name of Hakeem Olajuwon, who was quickly snapped up by the Houston Rockets. Stu had the big decision on who to take at number two.

Now I will let you know this, in hindsight the decision on who to take at number two is a no brainer, but at the time it was a very difficult decision for Stu, who happened to be very good at scouting and recruiting. He didn't have the blessing of knowing what we all know now. The previous year he drafted shooting guard Clyde Drexler from the University of Houston and a few years before that the man drafted Bill Walton! So when it came to the pick he had to trust he was doing what was best for the team and he decided to take center Sam Bowie and pass on a shooting guard out of North Carolina who would be taken at three by the Chicago Bulls and become the greatest basketball player of all time... Michael Jordan.

Wait, did I just say he had to pass on Michael freakin Jordan? It is comical to think about it now but trust me I have done my research and I have concluded that it wasn't as easy to see how great Jordan would be from up close in 1984. Stu missed the GOAT! The main reason why he missed Jordan was because of what he had done in 1983 by drafting Clyde Drexler. He already had two players that played M.J's position and in order to get him he would've had to let go of what was already in his hands.

We tend to think we would've followed Jesus at the mere sight of him if we lived back in biblical times. I sometimes think to myself if Jesus passed by me and said, "Abandon everything to follow me," I would risk it all for him and just follow. But I'm also realistic enough to be thankful that I live on the other side of the cross and I know what Jesus already did for me! I have spiritual perspective because of the Bible and can easily look through the pages and think, "Of course I would sell everything! I would have to follow this amazing man." I'm sure if Stu were alive today he too may say he would've made some trades that day to get Michael Jordan, or maybe he wouldn't change a thing, I don't know. All I know is that there are consequences to having something in our hands we can't let go of. It may hinder us from accessing the greatest thing we could ever have. That is the case with Stu in the '84 draft and the case with the rich young ruler in the Bible. They had too much to let go of and this made it hard for them to make the right decision—a decision that would be remembered for a very long time. The rich young ruler missed out on being a follower of Christ. He missed out on seeing the miracles that are not mentioned in the Bible and maybe writing an account of Jesus that would be called one of the gospels. Maybe his name was Ananias and we would have had a book of Ananias? Maybe he would've broken bread at the last supper and been in the upper room when the Holy Spirit came down? I don't know what he missed out on but I know he missed out. See, no one remembers the number two pick, Sam Bowie when pressed up against a name like Michael Jordan and Hakeem Olajuwon. No one even knows what the rich young man's name was let alone his significance in the world when pressed up against a Peter or a Matthew. I don't think there is a place you can go to today in the world and see a remnant of his wealth. It is gone and the consequences of following his true master is still the great consequence you and I could face: the consequence of missing Jesus.

CONSEQUENCE OF DEBT

"The rich rules over the poor, and the borrower is the slave of the lender." (Proverbs 22:7)

There will always be the consequence of a reliance to a master the more we serve it. In the case of the rich young ruler, he refused the invitation to become a follower of Jesus, and to my recollection he is the only guy who Jesus extended an invitation to follow Him and turned it down. His money stopped him from the one thing all his money couldn't buy—spending the rest of his life walking with Jesus. For some of us it may not be about missing Jesus but about being enslaved to our lenders.

The Bible warns us about debt. In my life I have seen how debt can make entire countries slaves to those writing the checks that are keeping them afloat. I come from Zimbabwe where the economy has been in tatters for decades and part of that is largely due to rampant corruption, looting by top officials, and bad debt management. I am not an economist or anything but I know from personal life experience that the lenders can start dictating how you go about every facet of your life. What probably hits closest to home for most of us is the issue of student loans. There is roughly $1.47 trillion in student loan debt in the United States. As I embark on my educational journey I am trying my best to not be part of that. I mean, if I had never been a trillionaire at some point in my life, this number may scare me but I've handled quadrillions before so I'm chilled. On the real though, how do you reconcile that figure? That amount is enough to wipe out Zimbabwe's national debt 91,874 times! Students owe a lot which means for a very long time to come, millions of young Americans will be slaves to their lenders. Biblically, that is not a good thing. This means until they can get themselves out of that hole, millions of people have acquired a temporary master, one which can tell them when they need to work and for how much. A master that can tell you to wear this t-shirt or you can't work here, or align yourself with this thing regardless of your beliefs or you will forever be in debt.

I'm by no means saying higher education is a bad thing but I am saying that we have to be wiser about how we tether ourselves to a master that is unrelenting and could possibly demand that we don't follow our true master, Jesus. The consequence of debt means that most young Christians believe they have to pay off their debts before they can be generous, and if you think about how long that normally takes, you can predict a less generous generation in the coming years. In turn, that means a less resourced church and a less aggressive force against poverty.

MONEY'S PURPOSE

In most of the sermons about this passage, including ones I have preached, I never hear why people think Jesus directs the man to liquidate his assets and give his cash to the poor. I mean we make it about the rich young man, or about Jesus exposing his motives, but never about where the resources are to be directed. Jesus doesn't say he must sell all he has and give Jesus the money so that He can give it to the poor. Jesus just asks the dude to sell his stuff and give that to the poor himself. I have looked at this passage over and over again and have wondered why the poor factored into all of this. If he sells everything he has and gives it to the poor, guess what, Jesus? He becomes poor! And how is that helpful to anyone?

This never made sense to me but after some careful thought there are a few conclusions we can reach. The first and obvious one is that Jesus cares about the poor! Simple and easy! There are people without resources and there is plenty to go around for all of us to live well. Like for real! If the world's wealth was distributed evenly, everyone would get $34,133. Crazy to think but that is not how the world would ever work, right?

In 2014, Wall Street got $26.7 billion in bonuses. That is a ridiculous amount of money. But it is classified as a bonus for hard work! Like extra! Let me put what that figure could do in perspective for you.

• It is enough to feed every American family (of four or less) that live in food insecure homes for a month.

• It is enough to provide school books for every college student in America for a year.

• It is enough to send 771,300 kids to college who otherwise couldn't afford it.

• It is enough to affordably house every homeless American.

It is a lot of freakin' money!

· · ·

Now I know what you may be saying: they worked hard for it so they deserve the bonus, so it's theirs to use as they wish. But the same could have applied to the man Jesus was talking to. The point that Jesus is confronting is the one we should all be confronted with when it comes to our stuff: if Jesus is our master then shouldn't our master determine how we live and how we spend? Jesus is essentially saying, "Dude, if I'm your master, then do what the master is saying." He challenges the rich young ruler to truly live out what he said. If you really love your neighbor as yourself, which is what you really mean by "all these I have kept since I was a boy" (Mark 10:20), then do for your neighbors what you have done for yourself and relieve their poverty.

The poor, the poor, the poor! Like I said at the start of this chapter, we are very selfish beings and we forget the poor. We can't imagine working hard day after day just for someone who didn't work as hard to benefit at our expense. That's why the people who hate social welfare hate it so much and that's why baby boomers constantly mock the participation trophy. People shouldn't get what they don't deserve! Then Jesus comes in and says, "Here you go humanity... for all your rebellion, for all your disobedience, for all your living lives contrary to God's Word—for all of that jazz you have done to me including murdering me on a cross—I give my life in exchange for your sin and rebellion. Oh, and you get to be children of God too! Oh, and coheirs with me!" Jesus is rich and he doesn't make us break a sweat to get what He was brutally ripped apart to purchase but instead He lavishly gives us what we don't deserve.

When we realize we were dead broke spiritually with no hope and we've been blessed beyond understanding, we have no option but to do the same to the world around us. No option! The response to Jesus pouring all that out for us is living a life poured out for others. If we have much, our response is to let others partake of what we have. Right now in the world there is a parent looking at a hungry child with absolutely no way to feed them. Like zero! Do you know what it feels like to look at someone you love and feel so desperate, so helpless, because you can't give them the most basic of human needs? Jesus grieves over our greed and lack of awareness. I tell you He looks at us scooping that food and leaving those fries and that half-full glass of water and says, "My child I have children who are dying for one of those or a sip of that." Please excuse me if I sound judgmental or rude but I really am talking to myself here. As I write this I can't shake off the fact that I don't want to just acquire more things and never consider those who don't have. I have enough stuff and I don't need more. We have enough, Western World.

Let us truly pray about how we can live a life that is different. A life that has the masterpieces God has created being taken care of rather than a pile of worthless plastic that brought us momentary joy that's only going to end up killing dolphins in the ocean. Generosity changes our hearts. There is some supernatural thing that occurs in our hearts when we are generous. I honestly believe we get a hit of dopamine when we do something for someone else or when we let go of something that is valuable for the sake of others. The world's problems always seem so impossible to meet yet if we all stopped focusing on ourselves and actually lived out the call to generosity we would see so much of the darkness lifted.

I don't want to dishonor God's Word by doing what Matthew 6 asks us not to do (go and read it) but I believe it is important to share what follows as a testimony. A few years ago I moved to the U.S. in what is a very long story (I wrote about it in another book—all about God's goodness, almost dying, getting a kidney transplant, and much more). It was when moving here with absolutely nothing that my family and I found ourselves totally dependent on the generosity of others for our day to day needs. An amazing family called the Wissingers took us in and we lived with them for almost a year. They clothed us, gave us food, and drove us everywhere. It was a crazy commitment to undertake on their part. They sacrificed so much every day in order to save my life. After a while we got all of our paperwork and we were finally allowed to drive but we needed to buy a car. It was simple, because all we would have to do was sell my and my wife's car in Zimbabwe and use that money to buy a car here. But then a whisper entered my heart in my time with Jesus: "Don't sell the cars. Give them away."

Now I don't know if that has ever happened to you but you feel like you've lost it when you first hear that. It makes no sense to give away cars when you don't actually have a car to drive yourself. But the more I prayed the more God made it obvious who I had to give the cars to and when the Spirit revealed who the person was, I knew this was for the transformation of my heart. My wife and I obeyed God and I have never regretted the twelve months we continued to live borrowing cars after we gave those cars away because my heart was truly transformed by that action.

Jesus wants our hearts more than anything. He does this because He loves us more than we could ever fathom and when our hearts have no other master they are free to truly surrender to His will and His ways.

THE HYPE

The money or the box.

There is nothing in this world that will ever tell you that the way to a better life is losing stuff. I mean minimalism may trend for a while and Marie Kondo could have her five minutes of fame here and there, but our greedy hearts just revert back to consuming. We so often can live like this life is all we have and that we ought to buy everything in sight to be happy. At the core of every marketing scheme and every HGTV show is a message that causes us to never be content with what we have. I grew up in the 90's and every rapper I followed was constantly projecting images of wealth and excess. The more the hip-hop genre grew the more expensive the things they flaunted were. Now we all, like the preachers who fall victim to the sneakers, feel like we need $600 Gucci sneakers to fit in with everyone else or that we need to drive a $200,000 car to have truly made it. I don't know what hype you're buying when it comes to money. It may be bigger houses or cooler countertops or maybe it's saving a certain amount of it so that you can retire comfortably. I hate to break it to you but there is a chance you may never get to see the days you worked so hard saving for and that's not me being a jerk, it's in the Bible.

We are all susceptible to buying the lie that the rich young ruler bought and the lie Adam and Eve fell into when they were in the garden. God says you can have everything except one thing and the enemy says the "except" is better than God's everything.

Growing up in Africa you always think, "If I can just get overseas I will have made it; if I can just buy Jordans then I will be happy; if I can just live in a place with no power outages and potholes then life would be full of joy." One thing coming to America taught me was that Eddie Murphy plays a terrible African and the dream America promises to bring is amazing from 7,500 miles away, but once you get here there are a whole different set of problems you have to face. You realize that potholes exist here too and you also realize that there are a whole different set of Jones' to keep up with.

Once you move to that neighborhood, or start hanging out at the country club you always dreamed of being a member at, or go to that elite school, you realize there is a new standard that you don't quite meet. There will always be a cooler, more expensive pair of sneakers; an easier to clean counter top; a nicer holiday destination; and a more elite school that costs just a bit more than you can afford. Unless you declare money isn't a master it will always try and master you. The hype will always be there.

THE HOPE

The everything that Jesus gives.

Here is the great hope we find in this story with the rich young ruler. Jesus loves us enough to confront us with the truth no matter how much it stings. He doesn't leave us thinking that we are complete when we still lack one thing. He also graciously puts something in each one of us to know at some level that we shouldn't live a selfish life. Maybe you are realizing this as you read and maybe, just maybe, you are confronting the other master that is trying to recruit you.

"Dad, mom, life in Zimbabwe is hard, right?" asked Hope, my daughter, the other day.

"Yes," we responded in unison. We were very curious about this little question that seemed to have popped out of nowhere. "Why are you asking?"

"I want to give away my Barbies to children in Zimbabwe," she said.

She then started to map out a whole missional plan to collect her Barbies and donate them to the children who had no toys. Her little heart was already saying "I have too much" and this convicted my wife and I big time. This five-year-old heart was already sensing the excess in her life. That thing Jesus places in all of us had been activated in Hope. "Share what you have, Hope," I imagine Jesus whispering to her, the same way He whispered to her mom and I to give away the cars; the same way He told the young man give away what he had and follow Him.

When we let go of our everything, Jesus has room to give us His everything—and His everything is way better than our everything. Hey, who knows, we may even see the stuff we gave up returned to us eventually.

My car story ends like this. As we were giving the cars away, God put it on a family's heart to give us their old car. But for some reason the car died and they couldn't do it. Unbeknownst to us, they too went and prayed and Jesus whispered in their ear, "Buy them a brand new car." For a year no one said anything to anyone else. They were waiting to hear from us and we were not really telling people we needed a car. The day we made the need known they came up and told us this awesome news they had been holding onto for a year! After awkwardly fighting them giving us this gift, they finally just gave us the check to buy the car and told us to bring the change if there was any. And that my friends is just crazy! Who does that? I know who! It comes from a heart that is following Jesus and not money. God only knows what happened to their hearts after that. All glory to Jesus! He is working out stuff in our obedience. He can see our hearts and He has access to the hearts of others too, some of which are fifty-years-old and some who are five-years-old. There is plenty to go around in the Kingdom of God and if we are all living open-handed lives and not getting stuck in the mole hill, we find that people are taken care of and the darkness of poverty is destroyed by those who love Christ.

ENNEAGRAM

When deciding what to tackle in this chapter I asked myself this question: "Rob, what makes you Rob Chifokoyo? Like, if you were to be dissected, what would be your key identifiers?"

"Well," I answered myself, "I'm a fun-loving, easygoing, heterosexual, Zimbabwean, black man."

Now you might not know that I'm heterosexual or Zimbabwean just by looking at me but if we spent just a little bit of time together those things would become clearly apparent. Over the next few chapters I am going to tackle the pieces that make us who we are. I will look at the hype surrounding those parts of us and hopefully point us to who we *truly* are.

The things that define who we are the most are those things our culture is wrestling with the most, especially when the Bible seems to be opposing popular culture. I know that there are potential cultural landmines here, so I will prayerfully endeavor to unpack these topics one piece at a time for these next few chapters, with as much love and grace as I can possibly amass.

THE ENNEAGRAM

It doesn't matter which direction I look right now, it seems to me that every single person is talking about the Enneagram. It's kinda like what Tebowing, Linsanity and the old person filter on that face app was—freakin' everywhere! All the freakin' time! Everywhere I turn I overhear someone saying, "Hey, I'm a seven, which means I like eating candy floss and partying all day!", "Well I'm a four and it's raining which means I'm in my happy place." If that's not overkill, all the sevens seem to be all over my Instagram stories trying to tell everyone they are a seven. So if this keeps trending in the right direction I'm just waiting for the "older" crowd to get a hold of this. It will be catastrophic to an extent I don't even want to imagine. Anyone remember when "they" finally figured out how to navigate Facebook and the excessive baby boomer FarmVille requests we all received? The Enneagram should not fall into the wrong hands.

Okay, so I don't intend to sound condescending but I am one of those people who doesn't like following the trend, which means I don't watch *Stranger Things* and only watched *Avengers End Game* on its last day in the cinemas. Oh, I cried at all the right parts, by the way, and regretted not watching it sooner but I will never admit that to my friends. (If you're wondering why I said this in this book, it's because my close friends don't read my stuff.) Back to the Enneagram... what was I saying again? Oh, I don't like following trends, I set them. If you're trying to figure out my number it should be somewhat obvious by the first five chapters of this book. I'm a seven. Yeah, I am an enthusiast.

You probably freak out if you come across anything that completely figures you out. It's like being on the streets of Hollywood and a magician asks you to pick a card, write your name on it, put it in your friend's backpack and then asks you to open your wallet and bam! Your card appears in your wallet, with the exact inscription you wrote on it. As amazed as you are in the moment, you are also freakishly freaked out by it, right? You think to yourself, "What else does this guy do and did he just snag my social security number in the act of doing this trick?" This is what it felt like when I first took the Enneagram seriously. I was blown away at the accuracy... to say the least it explained a lot. We'll talk about it a little bit more in this chapter.

CHARACTER DEVELOPMENT

I grew up in a home with five kids most of the year, but during the school breaks that number would rise to seven and sometimes eight if some of my cousins visited. Let's just pause and give a nod to my parents who undertook this madness year after year. I have two kids and I feel like I should be up for a Humanitarian of the Year award every year just for keeping them alive. So yes, eight kids was a lot for my mom to take on, yet I never once saw her complain.

Now in an environment with seven other kids you have to fight for every little bit of attention you can get, especially if you're the second youngest. So I became an attention-starved kid. I had over achieving brothers who were brilliant academically and athletically. I also had a sister who got attention, not for the things she did well but because of some of the difficult things she went through growing up. This left me and my little brother, and he was the baby in the family, so naturally he got lots of attention.

I, on the other hand, had to fight for it. I had to fight to be noticed. I had to come up with a story every day that was far more interesting than my brother's sporting and academic achievements or my sister's personal drama. So I assumed the mantle of the jokester, the one who could make everyone laugh. When I was about five-years-old I discovered that if I tightened my neck muscles I could make my voice hit a certain pitch that would send my family into hysterics. This high-pitched voice became my signature attention-grabbing tool. Every time I needed to get their attention I would mimic commercials or sing my requests in this high-pitched voice and they would all look at me. I had successfully, officially, become the family entertainer.

Even though I figured out how to do the attention thing at home, in the outside world I remained pretty invisible. At school, I found myself underperforming in the academic department due to my low attention span. And my athleticism wasn't much to write home about. So in sixth grade my parents sent me to a boarding school, about an hour away from where we lived. This school was awesome and I kid you not, it was the foundation for many good traits in me which I am still thankful for today. It was way better than any school I had ever been to, but I still remained pretty invisible. It was so bad the headmaster, Mr. Botha, called me Richard Chipoyera instead of Robert Chifokoyo for the two years I was there. Perhaps those two names seem pretty close to the untrained eye, I don't know, but in Zimbabwe those names are not similar at all! There was also the little detail of sewn name badges we had to wear that had our freakin' names on them! I felt so insignificant and after a while I actually started thinking he was saying my name wrong just to mess with me.

MOMENTS

You see, there was no way for me to get noticed in an environment largely based on academics and sporting ability. It wasn't high school where all you have to be is cool and be seen with cute girls to be popular. It wasn't like my home where I could just break out into a voice and make everyone laugh. Corporal punishment is a thing in Zimbabwe and cracking jokes in class was always at the risk of getting a sore bottom, and the pain for me wasn't worth the risk.

So I thought I would always remain unknown and plagued by the "what am I even worth?" question for the rest of time... until sixth grade camp in the mountains of Chimanimani. It would be in Chimanimani where Rob would finally find his voice! I mean, I found the heck out of my voice, you know what I mean? Some people look for their voice and never find it, kinda like Carl Lewis singing the national anthem at the 1993 Nets vs Bulls game. If you haven't watched that video on YouTube stop reading this and watch that performance. It is one of the most hilarious things I have ever watched!

Now, okay, Chimanimani '94 Outward Bound Camp. There he is, scrawny Rob Chifokoyo, who can't rock climb, who cried and almost peed his pants when he had to abseil down the mountain. But later that week I got a chance to redeem myself. We were placed in teams and had to create and perform a skit on the final night to get a prize. I remember, as we sat brainstorming what to do, a thought popped into my mind.

"Guys, I have the perfect skit," I told the group. "I have this thing I can do with my voice."

I clenched my neck muscles and did the voice for them and my team broke out in hysterics, just like my family had been doing for years. We knew we had a hit and we were going to center everything around me because of this voice.

You can imagine the element of surprise this voice carried when the audience first heard it! They had seen me for nine months and had no idea I could do this thing with my vocal cords. In the middle of our pretty dreary intro, at just the right time, out I came playing the *tokoloshe* (a mythological evil dwarf) in the mountains and uttered some unscripted words my memory can't recall. All I know is the crowd went wild! That night our skit won hands down and drew so many laughs it echoed in the mountains! Everyone wanted me to do the voice again! Including the prettiest girl in the school, Sarah Galloway! I was on top of the world! People actually wanted to hang out with me now, and not even to do the voice, just because I was me. Oh, and by "people" I mean girls. Yes, I was twelve... "people" definitely means girls. I had finally found this thing that got me noticed and it felt good. I felt like I had found myself.

There is this longing in our heart to be known, understood, and seen. The following year we got a new teacher who didn't know me and once again it was at another retreat where I would stand up, only this time by myself, and win the prize for the best story told at the camp. This time I didn't use the voice, just my sense of humor and good storytelling abilities. I remember my seventh grade teacher Ms. Drakes coming up to me and telling me if I wrote stories as well as I just told that one, I would be her top student. It was the first time I felt the affirmation of an entire audience encouraging me to stand up and speak. (I forgot to mention she was crying as she gave me the chocolate bar prize. She was clearly blown away.) I realized something that night... I can make people laugh. I didn't know where to place that or why I had such an insignificant, hard-to-place ability. Was I meant to be a stand-up comedian? Was I meant to make people laugh for the rest of my life? I loved making my brother laugh, it brought me joy. I loved doing the voice at the retreat and making my friends laugh at my sixth grade camp. I absolutely loved seeing Ms. Drakes' tears of joy and hearing Mr. Botha finally call me Robert, all because of that story. Making them laugh didn't take anything away from me, it actually made me feel full of purpose, like I was doing what I was meant to do.

Now I'm a pastor and I know my job is not to be a comedian when I preach but... I believe as a pastor I should always be myself and if I tried to fake a John Piper intensity or a Tim Keller seriousness people would sniff it out in a second. I would go as far as saying you can't actually successfully be anyone but yourself. I may even say you can't even if you tried. God made you special, with a purpose and a world that is waiting for you to walk in the fullness of your gifts.

WHO YOU ARE

The Enneagram, according to Ian Morgan Cron who happens to be an expert on it, is not meant to put you in a box but rather show you the box you're already in, and how to get out of it. If you haven't already, I would highly recommend you read his book, *The Road Back To You*. This here is not an explanation of the Enneagram but rather an exploration on the thought of what makes up our identity.

The book will help you see the Enneagram with a some-what Christian lens, and I say "somewhat" because I don't believe it's all dandy. But it is awesome!

According to the Enneagram, I'm a Type seven with a Wing eight, and that is already a very loaded sentence if you have any knowledge of it. If you have no clue what it is here is a basic overview of the types:

Type 1 – The Reformer (The Rational, Idealistic Type: Principled, Purposeful, Self-Controlled, and Perfectionistic)

Type 2 – The Helper (The Caring, Interpersonal Type: Demonstrative, Generous, People-Pleasing, and Possessive)

Type 3 – The Achiever (The Success-Oriented, Pragmatic Type: Adaptive, Excelling, Driven, and Image-Conscious)

Type 4 – The Individualist (The Sensitive, Withdrawn Type: Expressive, Dramatic, Self-Absorbed, and Temperamental)

Type 5 – The Investigator (The Intense, Cerebral Type: Perceptive, Innovative, Secretive, and Isolated)

. . .

Type 6 – The Loyalist (The Committed, Security-Oriented Type: Engaging, Responsible, Anxious, and Suspicious)

Type 7 – The Enthusiast (The Busy, Fun-Loving Type: Spontaneous, Versatile, Distractible, and Scattered)

Type 8 – The Challenger (The Powerful, Dominating Type: Self-Confident, Decisive, Willful, and Confrontational)

Type 9 – The Peacemaker (The Easygoing, Self-Effacing Type: Receptive, Reassuring, Agreeable, and Complacent)

When I started looking at this, I was so shocked by the accuracy of the test in defining some of the ways I acted as a seven and it made some of my childhood experiences clear to me. I wasn't just some kid who didn't have enough attention but it was a part of who I was. Even though I felt a little invaded it wasn't in a bad way at all, like it would be with the magician on the street I mentioned earlier. I realized I really was a fun-loving guy and I wasn't lazy in school, but rather I was just easily distracted! This too would explain how I'm writing a second and third book and yet I know no one else in my sixth grade class who has. I just needed the right interests, circumstances, and environment to thrive and I would absolutely soar like an eagle in the Drakensberg mountains! That's why I believe the Enneagram has been such a hit, especially in the last few years. It answers the question our culture and society are asking the most right now: who am I? We are in an age where we are struck daily on our timelines and newsfeeds with a new identity hot topic or a politician using identity politics to push their personal agenda. We want to be known and understood by others, but more than that we want to know and be understood by our very own selves. There is nothing more tragic than not knowing who you are.

There was a story in the news a few years ago about a man named Benjaman Kyle. Benjaman Kyle, if that is even his real name, was found next to a dumpster by a Burger King employee. He was naked, covered in blood, and with fire ant bites all over his body. The employee said it looked like somebody tried to kill him. To everyone's relief, Benjaman wasn't dead, but he was barely alive. He woke up almost blind with no memory of who he was. The only thing he seemed to know was this name with its odd spelling, "Benjaman". Benjaman, suffering from what had now been diagnosed as retrograde amnesia (also known as "Hollywood amnesia" due to its popularization in movies) was helpless. He couldn't get a job, a place to live, and he couldn't even get into a homeless shelter without any identification. It was only through the kindness of a nurse at the hospital that Benjaman had a roof over his head.

Can you just pause for a second and think about that? You wake up one morning naked and beaten, not knowing who you are. How devastating! The story went viral and everyone started to help Ben find out who he was. I mean the FBI ran his prints through their expansive database but nothing turned up. Dr. Phil even had him on the show trying to get this poor man national attention and still nothing turned up. No one knew who he was, no one seemed to be missing him, and no one seemed to care about it.

Even though we don't feel exactly like Benjaman, each and every human being has a sense of walking around with a need to be told who they are. Even if it's a test that can't be scientifically proven, we take it online and its results tell us we are a seven with a Wing 8. We need that!

THE HYPE

The other day I dared to suggest to someone close to me that I may be something the Enneagram says I can't be. I was doing this just to throw a spanner in the works. So I suggested I was a seven with a nine Wing.

"Oh no, that can't be!" I was told.

"Well, I'm turning into a four the more I follow Jesus," I said.

"No!" they replied. "Your main number can never change! That's not how the Enneagram works!"

So this thing that undeniably is an awesome tool also has these absolute rules that can't be broken, even by Jesus himself? Jesus can do whatever the heck He wants. This tool is not more powerful than the ultimate rule breaker. Jesus opened blind eyes. Rule broken! He just shouts "Eph-phatha!" and the deaf can hear. Rule broken! He says, "Lazarus come out!" and a stinking dead man walks out of a tomb! But... but Jesus can't make a seven into a four.

I was doing this to make a point to someone who totally agreed with me that our main identity can't be found in a tool that makes you do a ten minute online assessment. Our identity is found in a God that knew us while a strong swimmer swam toward an egg in the greatest rendezvous of our lives. When the race was won God began ENFJing the heck out of us! (That's a reference to the Myers-Briggs personality test, for those who don't know about that one.) He is the one who always knew who we were going to be and how we function under stress and security. He is where we go first.

There is a hype around using something like the Ennea-gram. I'm not trying to be all weird here, but it isn't all good. You do a little research and you find it has some spir-itual roots. Now this doesn't lead me to dismiss it, but rather to treat it like everything else around me with dodgy beginnings... with discernment. I went into a funk where I started to tell people who they were based on the Ennea-gram, more than anything else. My new found discovery of self was now being solely filtered through a number and what number I was when I was stressed and what number I was when I was secure, and what number everyone else was. For me and, I repeat, for me, I started to use it more than I should. The hype of the Enneagram is that it can cause us to trust in an identity that is created by a test with a logo that kind of looks almost like a pentagram (let's be real here) and we all know what that's all about. But hey, the Converse sign is a few points away from that too and I rock chucks all day. I'm not trying to mystify things that shouldn't be mystified, but I am trying to say I should be able to glean the good and watch out for my blind spots whilst refraining from departing from the truth of all truths, which is that I was known before I ever took the Enneagram and Jesus, who knows me completely, promises me in John 14:26:

> 26 But the Advocate, the Holy Spirit, whom the Father will send in my name, will teach you all things and will remind you of everything I have said to you.

I know sometimes He will use Ian Morgan Cron to teach us who we are and sometimes He will use some guy in Chile who may not know what the heck he has stumbled on. God is faithful. God is faithful. God is faithful. I have learnt the most about myself not from the Enneagram but rather from a five-year-old named Hope Paidamoyo. My daughter is my Enneagram coach because she is like a little mirror following me around constantly telling me, see this is what you look like when you pout over nothing; this is what you look like when you are stubborn; this is what your selfishness looks like. She also shows me the good parts of me that I'm also not willing to easily acknowledge. She shows me when given the right attention, I can excel. She shows me what compassion looks like and how beautiful it is to have a desire to help the least and the lost. She shows me other things that neither my wife or I possess because she is her own amazing little person, with completely new traits that God has formed in her. God is faithful. That is the point I am making here. Have fun with the Enneagram, by all means, but remember there is more to you. You are so vast and complex and you are going to enjoy the rest of your life discovering more about yourself than you can handle. This is where our minds should rest: in the truth that we are known fully and perfectly by our Father in Heaven.

THE HOPE

No matter how many times I hear Brené Brown speak on vulnerability, I still struggle with always trusting it is in being vulnerable that I am truly being strong. I know writing this chapter will probably be the most vulnerable I will ever feel due to some of the subject matter in today's cultural climate, yet something in me tells me it will be worth it. I am partially writing this book for other people but I am mostly writing this in obedience to God! Anything done with purity, in obedience to Christ, will always be worth it, even though we know the results will, not may, but *will* vary—thus making this the most courageous thing I have ever done. It is in being vulnerable we are truly known by others and we can truly know ourselves.

The story I told earlier about Benjaman's identity actually has a happy ending. After years of looking he was eventually granted a special identification card in Florida so that he could work. He was now officially Benjaman Kyle, with a job, a place to stay and a "normal" life. Until 2015, several years after he had been found, when a genetic genealogist from San Diego, Cece Moore cracked the case after working on it for two years. Moore discovered Benjaman's identity through a 1967 high school yearbook photo in Lafayette, Indiana. His real name was actually William "Bill" Powell and he had been last seen by his family when he was 28. Turns out he had a brother that still lived in Lafayette called Furman Powell. Bill, not Benjaman, was his real name and he had been missing for more than two decades. His new life had become somewhat normal but as soon as he found out who he was he left to go and live in Lafayette and be who he actually was.

Some of us are still looking in the wrong places to fulfill the longing of finding our true selves. We will go crazy every five years when a new personality test pops up while neglecting to go to the Father to ask the same questions we answer using online assessments. Have we ever asked God why we respond the way we do when someone gets a promotion? Have we asked God why we don't speak up when we are in a situation that clearly required us to? Have we asked God to not only make us more aware of His pres ence but to be more self aware in our daily lives? If you're like me, that is not what my prayer life looks like. I don't ask God to teach me things about myself and maybe we all should. Kids ask their parents stuff. Kids mimic their parents' attributes and they copy-paste a whole lot of stuff. Jesus copy-pasted His Father's whole script!

> 19 Jesus gave them this answer: "Very truly I tell you, the Son can do nothing by himself; he can do only what he sees his Father doing, because whatever the Father does the Son also does. 20 For the Father loves the Son and shows him all he does. Yes, and he will show him even greater works than these, so that you will be amazed. (John 5:19-20)

So are we asking the Father to show us how to love, act, walk, connect, and be in relationship?

Maybe that God knows you fully isn't enough for you to go to Him and ask Him to reveal to you who you really are. Maybe you have needed the assurance of other things to show you more of your true identity. My prayer is that you go to Him with your questions and requests. I'm not a conspiracy theorist or one of those weird Christians that think the Nike sign is evil, I just believe nothing created should ever overtake our creator in defining who we are.

Maybe you've forgotten who you are in Christ. The Bible, over twenty times, states who we are in Christ and all those can be found at hopeoverhype.com. I will focus on just one here.

9 For in Christ all the fullness of the Deity lives in bodily form, 10 and in Christ you have been brought to fullness. He is the head over every power and authority. (Colossians 2:9-10)

In Christ you are brought to fullness!!!

If you feel lost, or you feel your identity has bee stolen, I have good news for you! Jesus is the genet genealogist that reminds you of who you truly are. He the one who tells you that you're not Benjaman, you' freaking Bill Powell! You have a home, an identity and yo have a family! It is in Christ we find our true belonging an it is in Christ we find our true identity.

SEXUAL IDENTITY

We sometimes forget how important compassion is when we talk about things that don't affect us directly. As a society, we have forgotten how amazing relationships can really be if we don't enter a room with our minds shut off to other perspectives and points of view. So before diving into this chapter on sexual identity, I'd like you to place yourself in my shoes, so we don't misunderstand.

I feel compelled to write my thoughts and interpret what I read in the Bible as accurately as I can, and I'd like you to read my words knowing that I grew up in a country as a Zimbabwean male where same sex relationships were (and are) illegal. This makes me not only a novice in such matters but someone who is willing to learn more. I believe there are many people who will read this and some may take my words to mean something they don't and others will glean what is true and throw out what is not. I write this knowing that in today's climate this is a minefield, and many have been simply dismissed by others due to their beliefs, without proper discussion taking place. So with that said, I want to address the different people who may find themselves in a certain group around this issue.

TO THE LGBTQI AND POLYAMOROUS COMMUNITY

To you I want to say thank you for reading this. I know I do not have the right to expect you to read this, but you are continuing on, and for that I am thankful. I know I am going to get things wrong but you're at the center of a very toxic war on identity that I believe the church singled out unfairly. As one who is part of the group that did this, I want to say I'm sorry. We singled you out and muscled you out of our community without even listening to your hearts. We withheld grace, we didn't give space for hearts to wrestle with the Word of God, and more importantly, we rejected people under the guise of doing it in Christ's name. There is no one in the Bible that Jesus wasn't willing to hear out and there was no one in the Bible that Jesus didn't seek for. My heart is to speak the truth in love and possibly explain where I believe we have all gone wrong and should repent. All of us have lacked compassion and empathy at some stage along this journey. All of us have lacked tolerance for one another in one way or another. All of us have used anger and hate to drive the other out of town when we have had the power to do so. We all know that is true.

I want to say this loud and clear: *We are all made in th*

image of God. We all have areas we want to dwell in that the Bible tells us not to. We all have fallen short and are in need of a savior. Let us meet there, the place of humility, rather than the place of pride. If you identify with any of the groups in the heading above and also call yourself a Christian, then I know you know Jesus would have you read on with a loving heart toward the words put on this page.

TO AFFIRMING CHRISTIANS

I personally have to repent to you. There are times where I have dismissed you completely, blocked you out, and declared you as gone, never to be seen again. That was unlike the Jesus I follow. I never gave you an ear. I now know none of you woke up wanting to disrupt the system for the sake of disrupting it. I have to assume that the people I disagree with theologically were on their knees in prayer just as I want them to assume the same of me. I know you didn't just go, "Hey, let's wake up tomorrow and forget about the inerrancy of scripture, because wouldn't that would be a fun thing to do?" I know some of you have wrestled and tried to have conversations with people as to why you land where you land, and you found a door was never open to you. I hope you don't do to others what was done to you. I am inviting you to read along. I know there are times in reading this you will feel like shutting me off and maybe even mutter to yourself, "oh, here we go again," while rolling your eyes. I get it. I do that too. I am also giving you permission to skip this if you feel like it will affect how you read the rest of this book. The next chapter is really good! Anyway, you already bought the book and whether you read this part or not I will still be paying off my debts with your money (just joking!). I invite you to stick around and challenge my words but also to wrestle with them in prayer. I am a brother who is trying to be faithful, sharing a truth that is not mine, but belongs to the One who saved my soul, Jesus.

NON-AFFIRMING CHRISTIANS

Weirdly enough, I need to apologize to you too. I am not blind to how some of you, or should I say *us*, are trying to really be faithful in this. I know we have at times chosen the invisible corner and just hoped if we closed our eyes real tight and counted to ten everyone would get along. Or Jesus would come back. I know I will probably lose a bunch of readers by saying this but this is the group I belong to. I will share my thoughts in this part with a heart that has been radically loved by a Jesus who doesn't promise me happiness but rather promises me fullness in Him. We may be the ones who need to repent the most out of these groups and we may also be the ones who need to listen most. I believe there should be a million more books with a million more ways to say this but I am choosing the path of humility knowing there are many I love and care for in the first two groups above. I have prayed for them and God has continued to show me that i is my own heart I should pray for the most. The Word of God has clear warnings for all three of these categories, and I will share what those are.

I ask that we don't become a people that major in the minors and become the sort of characters that Jesus directed seven woes at in Matthew 23. Let us not neglect the more important matters of the Law like justice, mercy and faithfulness, as Jesus said. But Jesus also tells us not to *neglect* the Law. Repentance and humility are powerful things. Judgment and stubbornness on the other hand are not. This is not going to be resolved in a Facebook comment section and I know that the reviews on Amazon about this particular chapter from all sides are going to be character-building for me. I still press on, and choose to type with God's Word and love leading the way. I often say we should always speak truth but also realize that God is the one who changes hearts. Our job is to love those hearts without compromising our own walk with Him. I am also constantly reminded that God doesn't need me to defend Him. He's big enough to fight for Himself. He can handle it.

So with that all said, let's carry on.

SCENARIO ONE

Imagine your daughter came up to you and said, "Dad, I'm in love. This person fills my heart with joy and gladness and they take such great care of me. Dad, I felt so loved by you growing up and there is no one out there that makes me feel as safe, secure and as joyful as I did growing up like this person does."

As you hear her saying this you're trying your best to stay calm but inside you're overjoyed knowing that all the prayers you prayed for your little girl to find someone worthy of her heart have been answered.

Then things take a sudden turn. She changes gears and speaks in a voice that sounds like it is carrying the weight of a president about to push the nuclear button.

"I know because of what you believe, your role as a pastor and what I know of the Bible, that my amazing news is not all that amazing to you," she says.

A pregnant pause fills the room as you try and imagine the multiple scenarios which could possibly make this great news not so great. You try and break the silence with some light-heartedness and nervously utter the words, "What's wrong, is he a Baptist?"

She cracks a smile that your eyes have seen a million times before. A smile that has a hint of joy and all the weight of the world mixed in with it. You know at that moment you are delaying the inevitable. You know what she wants to say and you wish with everything in you that you could swallow her in your arms and say it for her. "It's a girl." The person she has described is another girl.

SCENARIO TWO

Imagine your daughter came up to you and said, "Dad, I'm in love. These people fill my heart with joy and gladness and they take such great care of me." Everything in the first scenario exists in this version of events except this... She's not in love with another woman but rather she is in a polyamorous relationship.

Wait, what?

You must be thinking where am I going with this? So I will explain. Due to the climate in today's culture we will read this next part through the eyes of a sexual orientation that has no hype around it. This is a group with many of the same dynamics that make up heterosexuality and homosexuality, but do not have the same support or attention around their cause. This evens the playing field and will require almost everyone reading this, except for the polyamorous community, to walk in someone else's shoes.

WHAT IS POLYAMORY?

Polyamory is defined from the roots *poly*, meaning "many", and *amory*, meaning "love". Polyamory is at its heart having many loves. Polyamorous people believe that it goes against their nature to be monogamous, which means they are involved emotionally and sexually with more than one person at the same time. Please hear as to why I am using these two examples. They have very similar arguments on almost every level. I mean socially, biologically and even more so, biblically.

Now I assume if you're not a Christian reading this you would say everyone should have the right to have sex and love whoever they want, and you wouldn't have a problem with polyamory. If you are an affirming Christian and believe that the Bible or Jesus is totally cool with my first scenario then you too should have no problem with this second scenario either. Why? Well I'll go into details later in this chapter. If you already stand in the space of saying you honor God's word no matter what, I also urge you to keep reading because this is by no means easy for you either. Jesus is an equal opportunity offender and we will go into the "because the Bible says so" argument by addressing what Jesus says about divorce later, which happens to be a topic we all have a close proximity to in the Church. Jesus spoke clearly about this topic as well and I will try and unpack as much of that too.

I was tearing up writing scenario number one, knowing the very events I was writing are filled with emotional complexity and have ripped hearts and families apart. I had been dancing with my five-year-old just minutes before writing that and I couldn't imagine how heavy the burden all the parties in that scene would be sensing in that moment. I wrote it knowing I have close friends whom I love who have been on either side of that conversation.

But I gotta be honest about writing scenario number two. I didn't feel that weight as much, if at all, to be honest. It's as if I can just dismiss the people who have had to have those conversations as unworthy of my compassion.

This may be an attitude that is carried by more people across this nation than we may like to think. They may dismiss the people who identify as polyamorous as "choos ing" to be sexually deviant, just like people used to do to the LGBTQI community only a few decades ago. Polyamorous people believe they deserve all the rights and freedoms that are being given to the LGBTQI community and, not only that, but they believe there needs to be a recognition by the Church of polyamorous Christians. So here is why you may not march with polyamorous people or stand up for them on social media and give them a month of celebration.

1. You don't believe it's a legit orientation, you think it's a choice.

2. You actually don't know someone who is polyamorous.

3. It's not on your favorite T.V show or your timeline.

4. Your favorite celebrity hasn't advocated for them.

There are reasons why we care about the things we care about. Sometimes those reasons are purely based on our feelings toward something and sometimes it's clearly because it's gone viral. Lions die everyday in Africa, but when the right people tell us to cry about Cecil, we cry about Cecil. Proximity and social awareness basically cover (3) and (4) above, so we're left with (1). It is in (1) and (2) where most compassion or empathy lives or dies. If we don't believe something is legit we immediately dismiss it. If we are not in close proximity to someone involved in it we also don't give it attention, as if it might not even exist, when, in fact, it does.

Some polyamorous people believe they were born that way. They believe that non-monogamy is not a choice but rather a default setting. Even though this is not popular, Consensual Non-Monogamy (CNM) is argued in many circles as a legitimate sexual orientation.

In Africa and Utah, where proximity to people in consensual non-monogamous relationships is high, you find that the Church is more confrontational to this lifestyle than it is to same sex relationships, because they don't encounter the latter much (if at all) due to the culture. So this is their culture war, so to speak. But when it trends and we are in close proximity to someone who expresses these feelings, it blurs the lines in our hearts. Culture and experience play a big part in our thought processes.

As I researched this, I realized the arguments Christian polyamorists make are almost identical to the arguments Christians in same sex relationships also make. Polyamorous Christians are saying that if you can essentially dismiss passages of scripture as being contextual then why not paint consensual non-monogamy with the same brush? I discovered three common arguments shared by polyamorous people that I want to address, because it serves as an example for the common arguments across the board—but it evens the playing field as polyamory is not such a hot topic in our media right now.

1. I WAS BORN THIS WAY, HOW COULD IT BE WRONG?

I empathize with the feeling of being born a certain way and being powerless to change it. There are many times in my early walk with God where I would wrestle with my natural passions as well. I got tired of fighting things that I naturally gravitated toward that the Bible called sexually immoral. I would ask myself, man, why can't I just look lustfully at a woman, just once? I mean why do I have all this sexual drive that I can't seem to overcome? What am I supposed to do with it? I'd spend days riddled with guilt because I'd feel like I'd let God down. Why do I have to suppress something that seems to be begging for an outlet?

Just because we are born feeling a certain way, it doesn't mean we are meant to act on those impulses. In a pastoral paper done by the Center for Faith, Sexuality and Gender, it says some affirming Christians say people are born gay therefore they should be allowed to express their love in the context of a consensual, monogamous relationship. In other words, God shouldn't (or wouldn't) punish people who were born gay, and they should have the right to a committed, monogamous relationship like everyone else.

But I think to myself, why honor the part of scripture that calls us to be monogamous but not honor the part that tells us to stay away from what it clearly defines as sexual immorality? To my knowledge, there is no passage in the Bible that calls us to monogamy outside of a heterosexual relationship. How do you even begin to want to honor one part of what the scripture is saying and not the other?

This is where, interestingly enough, polyamorists can have a compelling argument. I'm not trying to argue this to change your mind but to call those in disagreement with what the Bible says to actually ask themselves tough questions. If we make the argument that it's unfair for God to punish someone born a certain way or to have certain tendencies, why don't we also apply the same thinking about God to other things that we honor in the Bible that don't seem to be "fair" or "loving"? Why, for example, if someone feels they are an "angry person" and were born that way, is their argument not valid? It seems to me that being born a certain way should not be used as a means to justify living a life that is contrary to God's Word. Even the founder of the Gay Christian Network, Justin Lee, doesn't validate this argument. Rather, he says this.

Just because an attraction or drive is biological doesn't mean it's okay to act on... We all have inborn tendencies to sin in any number of ways. If gay people's same-sex attractions were inborn, that wouldn't necessarily mean it's okay to act on them, and if we all agreed that gay sex is sinful that wouldn't necessarily mean that same-sex attractions aren't inborn. "Is it a sin?" and "Does it have biological roots?" are two completely separate questions."

I have to be honest that sometimes when I hear people

say they were born that way I think to myself it sounds like they would choose another way, given the option. I don't mean to make that sound condescending at all but it's just a question I often think about when I hear those words. I had no choice in the matter... but if I did, who knows what I would have chosen?

I was born with what is called renal agenesis. My doctors told me my particular condition was also known as a pancake kidney. I found this out as I was fighting for my life in Zimbabwe as the sonographer was frantically searching for my kidneys after I had been diagnosed with end-stage kidney failure. As I was dying in a hospital bed days later, I had some thoughts about my situation. Did God's cellphone ring as He was forming me in my mother's womb and He forgot to drop the second kidney in there? Was God fully aware of how I was born? If yes, why was I born that way?

I bring up my birth defect not to argue that my kidney issues are the same as someone who was born with a sexual orientation, but to point out that there are a whole lot of people born with questions about why they are how they are. The one kidney thing happens more than you know. One in 750 people are born with one kidney and it is more common in men than in women. I could go on all day looking to blame God for how I was born, but as a follower of Christ that is starting the conversation from the wrong vantage point. I could start to list a lot of ways people are born that have way more catastrophic implications than my kidney or who people want to sleep with.

The thing is, whether people are born one way or not really shouldn't determine the way we act. Is God our master? If yes, then I follow Him and act the way He calls me to. We are born into a broken and fallen world run by a dweeb called Satan and there are things we will war with for a long time to come, including our sexuality.

> As for you, you were dead in your transgressions and sins, 2 in which you used to live when you followed the ways of this world and of the ruler of the kingdom of the air, the spirit who is now at work in those who are disobedient. 3 All of us also lived among them at one time, gratifying the cravings of our flesh and following its desires and thoughts. Like the rest, we were by nature deserving of wrath. 4 But because of his great love for us, God, who is rich in mercy, 5 made us alive with Christ even when we were dead in transgressions—it is by grace you have been saved. 6 And God raised us up with Christ and seated us with him in the heavenly realms in Christ Jesus. (Ephesians 2:1-6)

We will jump into this passage more a little later but it basically says this world has another guy who is pushing his own kingdom's agenda and the Bible specifically calls him the "ruler of the kingdom of the air." I think about all the dark sexual crap I've taken in through the airwaves over the years. I think of the hypocrisy and internal conflict that must dwell in the hearts of men and women who entertained images that pornography spewed out with women engaging in sexual acts with other women unrepentantly, only to wake up the following morning to condemn the same acts they were watching the night before. The fight we are in is the exact pizza we ordered. But hey, we were born that way. We were born with hearts that are riddled with an ugly hypocrisy due to the nature of the world we were born into. So whether it is the cravings of the flesh or the ungodly desires and thoughts we have followed, this BS is in the air literally and we either give in to it or we shut our screens and freakin' ask God to lead us not in the direction of the pheromones that pull us away from Him.

WHO IS IT HURTING?

In 1984, New York State passed its first seat belt use law. If you were caught driving without a seat belt on you would be fined $50. Today in the U.S., the "click it or ticket" approach has been adopted in almost every state with the exception of New Hampshire, which doesn't enforce this law for anyone over the age of eighteen.

The seatbelt law is really funny because if I don't wear one it doesn't hurt anyone except me. I mean if I choose to ride without one, who am I hurting? But whether or not you believe it is worth wearing one, the law is the law. If you get caught by a police officer without one on you will get fined and you will have to pay. He won't ask you to explain your beliefs in regards to seat belt laws. He will tell you this is the law, pay up and don't do it again. The law is the law. You may say, "Well Rob, the Bible is not a book of rules but it's about a relationship." I would say this back to you: "My marriage to my wife is not about obeying the rules. It's about relationship. In light of that, I tell you this... if the day ever came when I didn't feel like loving my wife and temptation to be unfaithful was knocking on my door, I would have to disobey the vows (the rules) I made to her on our wedding day to proceed. I would know full well that I was actively breaking something valuable."

You might say, "Well, Jesus did away with the Law." No, He actually didn't. He fulfilled it! In the seven woes in Matthew 23, Jesus actually told His disciples to be careful to do what the Pharisees say. He was insistent that we ought not to ignore the law but rather to honor it.

> Do not think that I have come to abolish the Law or the Prophets; I have not come to abolish them but to fulfill them. (Matthew 5:17.)

Following Jesus requires obedience and obedience is still a thing. We are not our masters but we live as people with a master. The logic that if it doesn't hurt anyone then it's all good is just not a good space to occupy. There are so many instances where there are consensual adults engaged in a sexual activity that even the most affirming Christian or the most tolerant society would not welcome with open arms at all. If you are reading this and you have used the terms "love is love" then all loves *should* be permitted. Affirming Christians, for example, don't seem to have a leg to stand on if they are not affirming way more sexual views than just same sex ones. I don't think you can ascribe to same sex marriage and same sex relationships being cool with God without also affirming polyamorous relationships. You have to be consistent in your love and not only give rights to, or fight only for, the people you are close to. Polyamorous relationships do not technically "hurt" anyone any more than normal relationships do. After all, "love is love", right?

I realize as I write this that my role in life isn't to tell people how they should live but rather to point them to the one who has the perfect plan for their lives; to point people to a loving savior that isn't waiting at the door ready to blast them with fire from heaven but rather took the blast on Himself in our place so that we could get in the door. But the danger for an affirming Christian is this: you are affirming something that you can clearly read in your Bible as being against God's design. Some even to the extent of recklessly celebrating what the Bible calls sin in the name of "love." That is not love on any level! If you know what is true and you choose rather to ignore it while you yourself are not standing in that space of disobedience you are actually cruel. You are essentially the guy that celebrates their friends jumping out of a plane without a parachute while full-on knowing that a parachute is required on the safety list. I believe that this verse is jarring for all of us who don't want to be excluded by the world due to our beliefs. When we long for friendship with the world above loving those in the world by giving

truth, we fall into a pretty dangerous space in God's Kingdom. Remember the sin we affirm is affecting the creation
that God so clearly loves and you are trying to stand
between God and His beautiful pursuit of those that don't
yet know of His love for them. We feel like we're doing
the right thing, the most loving thing by affirming, but
totally miss the fact that God is the one who sets the law,
not us.

> 4 You adulterous people, don't you know that friendship
> with the world means enmity against God? Therefore,
> anyone who chooses to be a friend of the world becomes
> an enemy of God. 5 Or do you think Scripture says
> without reason that he jealously longs for the spirit he
> has caused to dwell in us? 6 But he gives us more grace.
> That is why Scripture says:
>
> "God opposes the proud
>
>   but shows favor to the humble."
>
> 7 Submit yourselves, then, to God. Resist the devil,
> and he will flee from you. 8 Come near to God and he
> will come near to you. (James 4:4-7.)

The warning James fires off here is one filled with a
heartfelt call to turn away from the temptation of sacrificing what God has done for us in the name of acceptance
from the world. "The world" here meaning, of course,
human society apart from God. Then he wraps it up with a
"if you know, you know" statement in verse 17 that inclines
us to do the right thing.

If anyone, then, knows the good they ought to do and doesn't do it, it is sin for them.

Some of us know the truth deep in our hearts. There is an inner conflict. Those who believe Jesus sees homosexual lifestyles or polyamory as right, true and pure, wrestle with this more than they care to admit. Others have conflict on how to love such people. We need to admit that we are all struggling one way or another.

We are all struggling with God's fairness.

We are all struggling with our own desire to be loved and accepted.

And we are all buying into a message that says God died for temporary things.

These things I encourage you as a dear brother or sister in the Lord to pray through if you haven't already. I am not assuming you haven't prayed through these things, I am just saying that I know some haven't. It is a big deal to denounce something that is in scripture. Like probably the biggest deal you are going to ever deal with in your life. Each one of us is going to give an account of the way we lived and what we did or didn't approve with our words. Someday we will have to account for why we make the decisions we make, and if our reason is as lame as because someone else did or everyone was doing it, then we're in trouble. Buckle up, because the pressure on you to approve something is on its way. You have to have a strong conviction now rather than let peer pressure decide for you later.

The truth is the Bible does tell us who our sin hurts. And it hurts us.

20 When you were slaves to sin, you were free from the control of righteousness. 21 What benefit did you reap at that time from the things you are now ashamed of? Those things result in death! 22 But now that you have been set free from sin and have become slaves of God, the benefit you reap leads to holiness, and the result is eternal life. 23 For the wages of sin is death, but the gift of God is eternal life in Christ Jesus our Lord. (Romans 6:20-23.)

Jesus is the one who knows more than anyone else that the wages of our sin is death. He went through that death for us. There are some sins that have very clear symptoms that present themselves outwardly. We can't deny that such a sin is destroying us and we have to recognize that we can't keep going the way we are living. Then there are some things that don't seem destructive.

I didn't know I had a messed-up kidney until I was already dying. Not one day did I ever think to myself I should take note of how much sodium I take in or be careful to regulate my blood pressure. I just lived with this unknown condition inside me. Had I been made aware of it earlier, I could and would have been more vigilant. I don't know what made it shut down after thirty years of working fine, but like my doctor told me: "Rob, you have been unhealthy for a long time, but you just hadn't been sick yet." I was unhealthy but I just didn't present any symptoms. The wages of my condition was death and even though I'm in the fifth year of my life with a new kidney, still know there is a wage of death my condition will collect if I am not consciously living a healthy lifestyle.

We can choose to ignore the penalty of sin and refuse to turn away from our sinful life, or we can allow Jesus' credit card called Grace to pay for it and turn to a life in Him and His will. It is the silent killers like cancer or hypertension that are the worst diseases because when the symptoms show, it's almost too late. God's Word is the big "click it or ticket" billboard on the highway that informs us of the law, but it is also a credit card that could pay the fine we couldn't possibly pay if we choose to accept it.

IT HURTS GOD.

But our sin also hurts God. Sin really isn't about what we did or how we did it. Sin is more about whom the offense was against. We have sinned against God! It's written all over Numbers 21:7; Deuteronomy 1:41; Judges 10:10; Judges 10:15; 1 Samuel 7:6; Nehemiah 1:6; and Psalm 41:4. These are just a few of the many, trust me the list is exhaustive. So I will just focus on one other.

1 Have mercy on me, O God, according to your unfailing love;

according to your great compassion blot out my transgressions.

2 Wash away all my iniquity and cleanse me from my sin. 3 For I know my transgressions, and my sin is always before me. 4 Against you, you only have I sinned and

done what is evil in your sight so you are right in your verdict and justified when you judge. 5 Surely I was sinful at birth, sinful from the time my mother conceived me. 6 Yet you desired faithfulness even in the womb; you taught me wisdom in that secret place. (Psalm 51:1-4.)

It is in verse 4 after King David's sin is exposed when he realizes who he has sinned against. I mean realistically, David sinned against a whole lot of people when he jumped Bathsheba and killed Uriah to cover it up, but here he singles God out. He is essentially saying, "God I have hurt you by acting the way I did. My sin breaks your heart even if it doesn't affect anyone else." For that, David is clearly repentant and wholeheartedly wants to turn away from his sinful ways.

Our sin hurts God because it is against God. Mainly because He made us, loves us; but also because He sent His precious, only begotten Son to die such a brutal death so that we wouldn't be chained to sin. When we actively choose to cling onto the very thing God paid so high a price to free us from, it is grievous. Forget "love is love", God is the very embodiment of love. He loves big because He is love and He has chosen to love us with everything Our response when we choose sin over Him is like someone doing everything they can, including losing their own child to save you from something, and when they finally get to you, you just say no thanks, you shouldn't have! That would devastate anyone reading this and this my friends devastates our heavenly Father.

Does the Bible really say that it's wrong? Jesus never did, many say. But the answer is yes, the Bible mentions that same sex relationships and polyamorous relationships are sinful. (Romans 1:26–27; 1 Corinthians 6:9–10; 1 Timothy 1:9–10.) The argument that is made when people look at these passages is that it is Paul who is saying these things and the Church today doesn't adhere to everything Paul said. Some argue that Paul didn't read his Bible in context, thus allowing us to do the same. But we also have to recognize that Paul had a different responsibility. When Paul was writing his letters he had no idea what God was going to do with them. He was being inspired by the Holy Spirit to drop those lines. So if Kanye can say he "made Jesus Walks, so I'm never going to hell," then Paul can one-up that a trillion times and say he was writing Holy Scripture!

Here is the deal. You either believe the Bible is God breathed or you don't. If you don't then the thing you do on Sunday is shaking on a foundation built by kids on a short-term mission trip to Haiti. It's dodgy and is going to crumble as soon as the winds of popular culture blow through.

GOD BREATHED

16 All Scripture is God-breathed and is useful for teaching, rebuking, correcting and training in righteousness, 17 so that the servant of God may be

thoroughly equipped for every good work. (2 Timothy 3:16-17.)

So if all scripture is God breathed, it means every time Paul wrote a word, it was Jesus speaking through this apostle. He is not the crazy uncle in the Bible that no wants to have at their wedding but is being used by Jesus to communicate truth for us to be equipped for every good work. He is also, by the way, saying things that Jesus actually says.

Jesus spoke about sexual immorality in a way that everyone grasped. But even if He didn't, we condone all the other things He never spoke about too. He wasn't specific about a bunch of sins and was, believe it or not, incredibly specific about money. Does that mean that the way we view money is more important than abusive spouses? I mean, Jesus never mentioned that. Does that mean spouses should punch away because Jesus never said not to? The Jesus-never-specifically-said argument is not one we can take very far before it melts away like water ice (it's a Philly thing) in my two-year-old's hands on a hot day. I can guarantee you there were women who were in abusive relationships and marriages in Jesus' time on earth but there was silence from His end. Unless of course we take the logical step of knowing that there is no way the gospels are an account of every single thing Jesus said. The Bible even says that there isn't a book big enough to talk about all the things Jesus did (John 21:25).

If you read the Bible you will find that Jesus addresse

all sexual relations outside of the biblical context of marriage every time he mentions sexual immorality, as understood by the crowds listening to Him. He didn't have to spell out every single sexually immoral act by name in order to get people to understand what He was saying. He gave an overview. And I think there is more to be said here too. Jesus addresses other sexual immoral things that the Church doesn't seem too amped to address. Adultery is deemed a sexually immoral act and non-affirming Christians have easily picked apart the same sex, polyamory argument with scripture and yet have happily skipped over what Jesus says about divorce. Our inconsistency and blatant disregard for Jesus' words concerning this matter are part of the reason our hearts can't be seen in the other conversations we have concerning sin. We should honestly wrestle with areas in the Bible that confront our hot spots as well.

> 31 "It has been said, 'Anyone who divorces his wife must give her a certificate of divorce.32 But I tell you that anyone who divorces his wife, except for sexual immorality, makes her the victim of adultery, and anyone who marries a divorced woman commits adultery. (Matthew 5:31-32.)

Don't commit adultery? What is adultery? In this passage, if you read what is on the surface, it clearly says that marrying a divorced woman is committing adultery. For real? I can't count on both hands the number of loving, faithful people who fall in this category and yet that is what the Bible says.

Divorce is a hotspot. It's not easy to navigate what is and isn't permitted and yet it seems very clear what Jesus says about it. In verse 32, Jesus makes this point pretty clear. We often shy away from preaching this passage due to the sensitivity of the people who are living a life contrary to verse 32. We also struggle with it due to our proximity to people who we love, who may have married a divorced woman, like the passage says. We have to be willing to show that we too have areas where we have received grace and areas we wrestle with in our own biblical understanding. Honesty with our struggles and doubts is an important thing to have in our churches.

IT'S NOT FAIR.

"It's not fair" is what we may now all be saying after reading this. I agree, it doesn't *feel* fair. I have no idea what it is like to dwell in any of the camps I have spoken about. I have no idea who will read this book and what tone they will read it in. "Fair" is a complex word in the world of a Jesus follower.

If not getting remarried is not fair after cheating, then I guess God isn't fair. If it's not fair that you fall in love with someone of the same sex then I guess God is not fair. If God's fairness is not found in Him letting me have multiple sexual partners at the same time then I guess God isn't fair. Where else is God not fair in the Bible? Is it in

Genesis when He tells Eve that she will have pain during childbirth? I saw my wife give birth to two kiddo's and that seemed pretty unfair considering I was just standing there sort of holding an ankle. Was it Sodom and Gomorrah? Was it flooding the whole earth? Was it the prophets of Baal being smoked by fire from heaven? I look at all of those and then I think of the most unfair part of the Bible being found in one place.

> 11 Since, then, we know what it is to fear the Lord, we try to persuade others. What we are is plain to God, and I hope it is also plain to your conscience. 12 We are not trying to commend ourselves to you again, but are giving you an opportunity to take pride in us, so that you can answer those who take pride in what is seen rather than in what is in the heart. 13 If we are "out of our mind," as some say, it is for God; if we are in our right mind, it is for you. 14 For Christ's love compels us, because we are convinced that one died for all, and therefore all died. 15 And he died for all, that those who live should no longer live for themselves but for him who died for them and was raised again.
>
> 16 So from now on we regard no one from a worldly point of view. Though we once regarded Christ in this way, we do so no longer. 17 Therefore, if anyone is in Christ, the new creation has come: The old has gone, the new is here! 18 All this is from God, who reconciled us to himself through Christ and gave us the ministry of reconciliation: 19 that God was reconciling the world to

himself in Christ, not counting people's sins against them. And he has committed to us the message of reconciliation. 20 We are therefore Christ's ambassadors, as though God were making his appeal through us. We implore you on Christ's behalf: Be reconciled to God. 21 God made him who had no sin to be sin for us, so that in him we might become the righteousness of God. (2 Corinthians 5:11-21)

The most unfair part of the Bible is God giving His pure Son, whom He loves, to suffer a brutal death handed to Him by the creation He made. Jesus didn't owe me anything and He went through with the deal. All the junk I had done to create the great chasm between God and I was restored on the cross. Was it fair? Absolutely not. Yet Jesus went through with it leaving me nothing but grateful. Even if nothing else goes my way for the rest of time, knowing He did that for me is more than enough. More than enough! His unfair death relinquished my right to any other fairness because there is nothing the Christian heart should not be willing to give up for His glory!

THE HYPE

We all want to belong, and when a group of people constantly tell us we don't belong, we look until we find those that say we do. The hype around sexual identity is all about belonging. Here is a flag, a month, and a community. Community is a beautiful thing and not having one is devastating. There is no struggle that the Church should not be willing to welcome. None. Jesus engaged everyone who came to Him regardless of struggle. It doesn't matter how I belong as long as I belong. Who you choose to sleep with should never be an identity you so strongly belong to that you are willing to dismiss everything you have loved and cared for. Who someone sleeps with should not be an identity that allows you to expel them out of your life, love and care. But sexual identity as a main identity is a cheap identity. You are more than who you love. You are more than the sum of your earthly desires. You are more! Maybe you believe you were born a certain way... the good news is in Christ we are born again! The passage above says in verse 17 that we are *new* creations in Christ. Jesus makes us brand new. Not only that, He gives us a community that loves and honors Him—that doesn't leave us on our hard days but goes the distance. That is just like the Cheers intro song, "Sometimes you wanna go where everybody knows your name and they're always glad you came." That is what a community of followers is. We love hard and we don't compromise and we never leave. We will always be there by your side. But the unfortunate bit is, this is not how it is now, is it? We don't love as hard, we sometimes compromise, and we do leave. That doesn't negate the fact that the Bible tells us to love no matter what.

THE HOPE

We all have a preexisting condition and there was no insurance company that was willing to take us on. We were all doomed until God flipped the script on the enemy on Calvary and swooped us up out of our pit of sin. He was the insurance company that said, "Not only will I take you on with your preexisting condition, but I'm going to heal you." He did something amazing! Salvation is a beautiful thing, my friends. We were undeserving and God saw it fit that we find our identity in Him. He bought out our contract to sin as stated in 1 Corinthians 6:20 and gave us a new found freedom in Him. He shows us what we were designed to be.

> 12 "I have the right to do anything," you say—but not everything is beneficial. "I have the right to do anything"—but I will not be mastered by anything. 13 You say, "Food for the stomach and the stomach for food, and God will destroy them both." The body, however, is not meant for sexual immorality but for the Lord, and the Lord for the body. 14 By his power God raised the Lord from the dead, and he will raise us also. 15 Do you not know that your bodies are members of Christ himself? Shall I then take the members of Christ and unite them with a prostitute? Never! 16 Do you not know that he who unites himself with a prostitute is one with her in body? For it is said, "The two will become one flesh." 17 But whoever is united with the Lord is one

with him in spirit. 18 Flee from sexual immorality. All other sins a person commits are outside the body, but whoever sins sexually, sins against their own body. 19 Do you not know that your bodies are temples of the Holy Spirit, who is in you, whom you have received from God? You are not your own; 20 you were bought at a price. Therefore honor God with your bodies. (1 Corinthians 6:12-20)

Our new contract releases us from the bondage of sin but reinstates the life-giving atmosphere Adam and Eve found in the garden. We are now free not to:

• Do whatever we like. (Verse 12)

• Be mastered by sin. (Verse 12)

• Use our bodies to be sexually immoral. (Verse 13-18)

Not all sins are equal but sexual immorality is more than just same sex relationships. Sexual immorality is sexual immorality. All of them offend God but this particular one wounds Christ in us. Our bodies are members of Christ himself. This passage encourages us to flee from it. Run! Our prayer shouldn't be to stand in the face of sexual immorality but rather to be given the strength to flee from it. The hope of all hopes in this is that we don't have to anchor our identity in our sexuality. If we were bought by God and set free from sin then let us walk in that freedom.

Perhaps you have struggled with your sexual orientation for ages. Perhaps you have struggled to find a home that accepts you. My prayer is you find followers of Christ that will be listeners that will love you ferociously and walk with you in truth until you are free, whatever that freedom looks like. You may have this battle with you for what feels like for ever but our response should be that you will always have a loving community with you each step of the way. In eternity we will all be free from all the crap that plagues us. Free from all our inborn stuff that the enemy pounced on us to try and tear us down the moment we opened our eyes in this world. The only label we should be willing to wear is the one that says "child of God" and, in brackets, (still working out a bunch of things.) Jesus bought you back from all the other identities to give you this one. He travelled the greatest distance and dealt with all the rubbish that this earth had to throw at Him to save us. We dare not say, "Thank you. Next!"

NATIONALISM VS PATRIOTISM

Coming to America was one of the most surreal experiences I have ever had in my life. I arrived at L.A.X. in 2007 after the longest flight I'd ever taken, feeling like Christopher freakin' Columbus! Four visa denials later, I mean four attempts at $200 a pop, and I was finally here! As soon as I cleared customs I felt like shouting out in my Dave Chappell voice something I'm not inclined to put down in writing here. I remember going over to baggage claim, collecting my bags and proceeding to go to a public telephone (if you remember those) and calling my brother in Virginia. "Dude, I'm in L.A!" or "Iwe, Cowfonya," which is what "California" sounds like in my Shona accent.

Then it hit me right in that moment. This place looks a little bit different from what I've seen in the movies. It didn't look like *Beverly Hills 90210*—I mean where all the whities at? All I could see were hispanics with sprinklings of chocolate and a splatter here and there of an asian or two. For real. I think the first white person I saw was the guy who came to pick us up. This America was a little different than the one Dawson's Creek had shown me for all those years. Where was Chandler, Monica, Phoebe, etcetera? All I could see were people who looked like Cruz Castillo from the hit 80's soap opera, *Santa Barbara*. If you don't know what *Santa Barbara* is, just know it still disappoints me quite incredibly that not a single American I have ever spoken to has even heard of the show.

This was my L.A.X experience. A different America. Not a bad different, but just different.

It was the next morning when the America around me took a complete 180 degree turn. I woke up in Orange County and thought this place looks a lot more familiar. I mean this place was whiter than Ed Sheeran wearing a white suit in the middle of a snow storm! It was so clean I was convinced you could lick the streets and still be fine. The air smelt different and the birds seemed a little happier over here. The dogs... I mean the dogs had it made. They were rolling in freakin' strollers and were wearing sunnies, for crying out loud. I was convinced when dogs die they don't go to heaven. No my friends, when dogs die they are reincarnated in Orange County. The O.C had also been popularized globally by the countless MTV reality shows based in the area and of course the hit teen T.V show, The O.C. Man everything was just like the show. America was beautiful!

As we drove around I started to notice something I had never seen in Southern Africa before. The only time really saw Zimbabwe flags was outside a stadium before a big game. But here I noticed in those first few days in Orange County that to see an American flag posted outside of someone's front door was commonplace. Was it Independence Day? I wondered. Was the U.S. playing some other country in baseball? (This was before I found out the World Series is not really open to the rest of the "world.") My flag experience went beyond porches and front doors and moved to peoples' clothes. It wasn't out of the norm in those first few days to bump into someone wearing an American flag shirt or shorts.

It was so odd for me to experience this. Not in a bad way at all, but I had just seriously never seen this display of love for a nation before. Americans were fans of America and why wouldn't they be? I mean, if the birds could rock American flags too, I'm sure they would go for it. Tustin, Orange County, California was the happiest place I had ever been to! It was very different from back home in Zimbabwe. Like *very* different! The guys back home who were super proud of the flag were the crazy, radical, militant government extremists. If you were to bump into someone wearing the colors of the flag in Zimbabwe in 2008, you were seconds away from being asked to say the ruling party slogans and failure to do so would result in a beat down. So my mind took some time getting around to fully appreciating how to take all this pride in. Once I did, realized this national pride wasn't harmful at all but rather convicting. Rob, why don't you love your country this way? I asked myself. Would you wear your national colors around on a random day or are you embarrassed to be associated with your land? After all, we only have one home we can belong to and if you don't love it, who will? My memory remembers feeling this but to keep it one hundred with you, I don't know if it went on for minutes or seconds before being abruptly interrupted by my prevailing recurring thought during that trip... which was to make sure to eat that Wendy's Burger thing again as soon as possible.

I believe there are two extremes when it comes to what we define as nationalism, and that God wants us to land somewhere in the healthy middle of these two. There are people who have absolutely no pride in the nation they're from and only see the nation where God placed them as being something to be ashamed of. Then there is the other extreme, which is those that see their nation as a god. This is the pure definition of nationalism. This viewpoint has the power to eliminate our ability to honor and obey God if the two ever came to odds with each other. You may be thinking how does this happen? Well if we place anything above God and it sits on the throne of our hearts I believe God's Word will be at odds with it at some point. Which is why it is important to fundamentally understand the difference between nationalism and patriotism. Nationalism and patriotism are two different things that are often confused for one another and I believe that God wants us to be patriots rather than nationalists.

NATIONALISM VS PATRIOTISM

Nationalism as defined by the Merriam-Webster Dictionary is this:

> loyalty and devotion to a nation
> especially : a sense of national consciousness exalting one nation above all others and placing primary emphasis on promotion of its culture and interests as opposed to those of other nations or supranational groups.

Patriotism is defined by the Merriam-Webster as

> love for or devotion to one's country.

These have often been confused with one another. Before writing this book, I wasn't completely aware of this myself. The difference between the two lies in the fact that nationalism starts with patriotism's core but then takes it extreme, turning into a version of love for a nation that separates, attacks, and destroys others. I believe there is no way God is asking us to not love our home. There is a beauty in loving where you're from. But God is calling us to not love that place at the expense of loving Him and others. See, if anything causes us to not love our neighbor *as ourselves*, meaning what we would do for us we do for others, then I believe it doesn't have God's endorsement.

LOVE FOR MY HOME

Zimbabwe is a beautiful place that lies between the mighty Zambezi and Limpopo rivers. As I think about describing what it's like, I'm dumbfounded as to where I could possibly begin. The weather, oh the weather is always amazing. I didn't appreciate the weather until I had to shovel snow. Let's just say there had never been a day in my life where nature made me work so hard to get out of my own home. No matter what direction you head out in Zimbabwe, you are always going to experience her beauty. There is no Nebraska in Zimbabwe (no offense, Nebraska). From its amazing array of nature to its majestic crown jewel, the mighty Victoria Falls, you will be awestruck at every turn.

Zimbabweans are also an amazing people. Friendly, always smiling, incredibly accommodating and always willing to put the needs of others before themselves. These amazing, peace loving people are the most adaptable, resilient and hard working people I have ever met. They have a way about them, a kinda Zim swagger we proudly call "Zwagger", and no matter where we land on this planet we can thrive. I love Zimbabwe. I am proud to be Zimbabwean. I AM ZIMBO to the core! This is the part where people usually say that even though it's not perfect I still blah blah blah... I am not going to do that. I am actually going to lovingly tell you the things I don't love about my nation.

Zimbabwe (dzimba dzemabwe) literally means "stone

houses" which refers to the fortified stone fortresses built by the Rozvi. I won't go into all of it but the dominant Shona tribe built a city of stone and at the height of its power in 13th and 14th century it was a major hub in the region for trade. The ruins of this fortified city of stone can still be seen today in what is now called "Great Zimbabwe", which is a world heritage site. Zimbabwe, which is an extremely mineral rich country to this day, was churning out as much as a ton of gold per annum during that period. This is important to know in light of what ends up happening in Zimbabwe's future. At some point the Shona's fortified city of stone was destroyed and Zimbabwe and her riches were at the mercy of outsiders. Fast forward this period of time to the emergence of colonization and the trajectory of Zimbabwe and her people starts to change drastically. This is largely due to the arrival of a young British mining entrepreneur called Cecil John Rhodes who pens a mining deal with the then King of the region, Lobengula, in 1888.

The deal didn't last and by 1893 Cecil is given a pretext to go to war with Lobengula and this, ladies and gentlemen, is how the beef gets beefy. The people who had come to mine gold stumbled upon more than they initially imagined. They decided that they needed to have control over this and fifty years later the European population in Zimbabwe rose from the initial mining crew to 220,000 white settlers!

It was in the 50's when the majority black population found a political voice and started to stand up against decades of being steamrolled by the colonialists. At this time there was a white superiority culture established in Zimbabwe (then called Rhodesia) and they were not in any way willing to have the potential of a black majority rule in the future. It was also during this time when the two dominant black tribes, the Shona and the Ndebele, established political parties and leaders. Joshua Nkomo, a Ndebele, emerged first as the leader of the local chapter of the ANC (African National Congress, which is the ruling party in South Africa today, led by Nelson Mandela). But this caused the Rhodie's (white Rhodesians) to ban this party which forced Nkomo to start something totally separate. Nkomo gathered other leaders into this party called ZAPU, among them Robert Mugabe and Ndabaningi Sithole. The latter left Nkomo in 1963 and formed ZANU, and this led to decades of persecution and politically motivated wrongful arrests. Mugabe spent ten years in prison but it was in prison where he educated himself, thoroughly, emerging with two law degrees. He was more motivated than ever to see a free Zimbabwe. It was in the 70's that he led a successful guerrilla war against Ian Smith's Rhodesia and led Zimbabwe to independence in 1980.

In the paragraphs above there is a deep seated incubation of racism and brokenness which was certainly never dealt with to the point of healing. Until this day this affects black and white Zimbabweans, both young and old. There is post war trauma that was never ever addressed. In those paragraphs, deals were dishonored; allies betrayed each other; there were assassination attempts; loss of loved ones; exploitation of the poor; and destruction caused by unhealthy self interests. There too lies the things that make up the things I do not love about Zimbabwe. In there lies the roots of the corruption I saw growing up, the racial discrimination I faced and the injustice Africans face today. My thoughts on calculating the labor and wealth taken out of Zimbabwe to build other nations and their constant refusal to be even the slightest bit accountable as to how debt in African new democracies is created, infuriates me. What makes me even sadder is seeing what these liberation heroes turned into when given the chance to make the lives of fellow black Zimbabweans different. The same people who were wrongly imprisoned and suffered much for freedom turned into the monsters that hunted them and inflicted the same treatment on their own.

They took productive farms that had made this beautiful land the beacon of the region and irresponsibly distributed land among themselves without the slightest care how this would affect their fellow countrymen. They drove the economy into the ground and watched poverty suffocate their own as they passed by in their expensive, luxurious European cars. They sowed seeds into the European automotive industry to appear as those who had "made it" while they ignored the very industry which sustains the land they live in. They watched as the Zimbabwe they fought for disintegrated before their very own eyes, because of their very own actions. I say all that but I don't just blame them for how they turned out. They were absolutely a product of their environment. The world and the Church need to take a moment and realize there are reasons people end up being the way they are. Sometimes this is caused by trauma and abuse. Others times it's caused by neglect and unhealthy practices that have been passed on generationally. This is how oppression, racism and corruption breeds. It is modeled for others to see.

During the war for liberation in the 70's there are accounts of Selous Scouts (white special forces soldiers) entering villages with their faces painted black so that they wouldn't be detected at a distance. They would ask in perfectly fluent local dialect if there were any ZANU fighters and if they found out the village was harboring ZANU freedom fighters there would be hell to pay. One account of what these squads would do was they would line up the whole village lying face down on a local soccer field, and I mean the *whole* village. They would then proceed to drive back and forth over their lined up bodies in their all-terrain combat vehicles (called Pumas) crushing body parts until the cries and screams stopped. A woman who gave an account of her experience of this said all you could hear was the sound of children crying, smooshed body parts and bones breaking... and there was nothing you could do to stop it. Your only hope would be that maybe you and your loved ones would just get broken arms and legs.

Can you imagine surviving that? Knowing that these guys drove over your children just so they could conserve ammunition? Then try and go a step further and imagine after that war going to work as a farm hand, and getting treated as a lesser human being for the next two decades by the man who was possibly responsible for doing that to your family? You won the war, but you're still dirt poor and the guy who ran over you became more successful in your own land. I know that many lives were lost on both ends of that, both black and white, but there was clearly one oppressor; there was clearly one denying the other of their rights. That is the complexity of Zimbabwe. That was why the majority population lacked a level of empathy when the white owned farms were being invaded. The liberation leaders never dealt with their memories of the ugliness of war. Products of bitterness, numbing pain with material things, living free on the outside but still captors in their own minds.

All the undealt-with stuff meant that Zimbabwe became a nation that looked like it was over its pain but really wasn't. And so the inevitable happened. Corruption begets corruption and before we knew it, we barely had the most basic of commodities. It got so bad that you even had black people who lived through the war saying things like, "Even when the whites were oppressing us, things weren't this bad," or "At least we had electricity, water and our trash was collected." Things were terrible and at the height of its economical problems, Zimbabwe had the worst inflation rate recorded in the history of measuring inflation. It feels surreal when I tell people that I used to be a quadrillionaire (which, based on the red squiggles under the word when typing, my computer won't even acknowledge that is a real thing).

In this part, my prayer is that we can be honest about

our love for a place without ignoring the ugly parts of it. We often think that just because we love something we have to ignore what is messed up about it. But that is false. I believe that if you love something, you are inclined to be more honest about the darkness of its past and how to avoid history repeating. When we are honest about the broken state of our beloved land we can now see what needs to be done to fix the brokenness. We can now cry out to God and ask him for a solution to the problems our nation faces.

I believe that a healthy love for your nation is not one that ignores the darkness in order to elevate the image of your country, but rather one that first and foremost has a heart and a desire to acknowledge and restore the brokenness. We see this in the Bible countless times. There was a man who was a shining example of this. Nehemiah 1 reads.

1 The words of Nehemiah son of Hakaliah:

In the month of Kislev in the twentieth year, while I was in the citadel of Susa, 2 Hanani, one of my brothers, came from Judah with some other men, and I questioned them about the Jewish remnant that had survived the exile, and also about Jerusalem.

3 They said to me, "Those who survived the exile and are back in the province are in great trouble and disgrace. The wall of Jerusalem is broken down, and its gates have been burned with fire."

Nehemiah inquires about home from a group visiting

him in exile from Judah. His brother doesn't initiate the matter but rather out of concern and care for his home and his people, Nehemiah asks how everything is going. His brother tells him things are bad, dude. Home is broken down and the people are not only in trouble due to their vulnerability to attacks but they are also disgraced.

I resonate with that as someone who has a love and concern for Zimbabwe and Zimbabweans. We have suffered much in our nation and many have had their pride and love for country ripped away from them. You only get to have one home to belong to. As an immigrant in the U.S., I know that this is not my home country. I am reminded of that almost every week and in some instances, every day, especially now that immigration is a much publicly addressed matter. You only have one home and mine is Zimbabwe.

You know there is something about home. Home is where you get to just walk in the kitchen and eat a handful of Cheerios when you want. Home is where you can prance around in your boxers and whoever doesn't like it has to deal with it. Home is where you get to just be you. There is a freedom about home that is unlike any other. I ask people who are transplants from other states about their home town and they can't tell me enough about it. The people from Florida always talk about Publix and how that is like the greatest grocery store in the world. They talk about it in a way that makes you want to go to such a gangster grocery store. "Publix with an x", they always emphasize, as if almost to say, "Don't get it mixed up with any other." They don't care that it's weird, it's home. The people from Georgia will tell you all about Zaxby's! They will even commit what I would call culinary blasphemy and say the Zax sauce is better than Chic-Fil-A sauce! What? That is absolutely not true because there is no other sauce above Chic-Fil-A sauce. In the world of sauces there is one name above them all, can I get an amen? I can't blame them though... it's home! When I talk to people from New Jersey... let's face it, if you're from New Jersey, you're lucky you got out! (I'll pay for that some day!) The point is home is home.

Home is also familiar. Like when I'm in Zimbabwe I don't have to tiptoe around things. I don't have to wonder what someone is thinking or how they would respond to something. I back myself because I'm from there. Whereas here, I sometimes feel how I feel when I'm in a hotel room. I always ask myself, "I wonder what went on in this very room last night." I wonder what happened in that very shower! It's not that home is perfect or cleaner it's just that I actually know the one-year-old that pees in my tub. We have a relationship, and it is because of that relationship that makes our home just that—home.

Nehemiah hears this news about home and it breaks his heart. He knows that this is not how his home should be. So he confronts the darkness. First, he does this through prayer. He goes through a weep, pray, love in verse 4 of Nehemiah 1.

When I heard these things, I sat down and wept. For

some days I mourned and fasted and prayed before the God of heaven.

Nehemiah's response to the news is to weep over the brokenness. This cupbearer to the king that lived 800 miles from this mess didn't just go, "I'm good. They can take care of themselves." He wasn't a hotshot back home and it wasn't his obligation to do anything. You know the thing about tears and weeping over brokenness is that it's a spiritual thing. There are very few places on the planet and, I mean places, not people, that I have wept for. There is something supernatural that happens in your heart when you are brought to tears over your nation. It's something I can only describe like a wind that comes out of nowhere and sweeps you away with it. I saw this happen in the life of my youth pastor, Pastor Evan, a few years ago, and to this day I still can't wrap my mind around it.

RESTORING PRIDE IN YOUR NATION

On April 18, 2016 Pastor Evan Mawarire was struck by a strong conviction that compelled him to say a few words about a nation he loves. He thought, I must make a video, like most of us think when we are sitting alone and have a thought pop into our heads that we feel our friends must all see. Only that this wasn't a thought about a trade that had happened on his favorite sports team or a critique of a performance he had just been watching on T.V. No, this... this was something very different. See, earlier when I spoke about Zimbabwe, I shared that after the liberation struggle there had been a sort-of smooth transition of power that gave Zimbabwe about a decade before the turbulence of economic strife started to be felt.

It was in the mid to late 90's that the effects of decades of corruption started to reverberate around the country. Through mismanagement and failure to correct the already spiraling economy, coupled with bad policy decisions, Zimbabwe was well on its way to imminent destruction. So it was on this night after decades of rot, broken dreams, brain drain in the region and multiple changes of currency that Evan pulled his phone out as a big *PFUTSEKE* (a socially accepted expletive in Shona) and wake up call to those that were in power. The video started with him leaning into the camera with the Zimbabwean flag wrapped around his neck like a scarf. His phone seemed to be propped up at an angle that made the moment seem more intimate.

It was like he was about to tell us a secret. Then the following words came out of his mouth.

THIS FLAG

This flag,
> *This... This beautiful flag.*
> *They tell me that the green is for the vegetation and the crops,*
> *I don't see any crops in my country.*
> *Hanzi the yellow, hanzi the yellow is for all the minerals,*
> *Goridhe (Gold in Shona), diamonds, platinum, chrome,*

I don't know how much of it is left,

And I don't know who they sold it to and how much they got for it.

The red,

The red, the red, the red they say that is the blood.

Is the blood that was shed to secure freedom for me and I'm so thankful for that,

I just don't know that if they were here, if they were here they that shed their blood

And saw the way that this country is that they would demand their blood be brought back.

They tell me that the black, the black is for the majority, people like me.

And yet somehow I don't feel like I'm a part of it.

I look at it sometimes and I wonder is this a story of my future or is this a reminder of a sad past?

Wherever I go and I put on the colors of Zimbabwe, they look at me as if they want to laugh; they ask are you from Zimbabwe? Vachiseka (Laughing in Shona).

Sometimes when I look at the flag it's not a reminder of my pride and inspiration it feels as if I just want to belong to another country.

This flag.

So I must look at it again with courage and try and remind myself, that it is my country.

I look at the green and I think to myself it is, it is not just vege-ation, but the green represents the power of being able to push through soil. Push past limitations and flourish and grow. That's me, my flag.

The yellow, yes it's about the mineral but not just the minerals in the ground but the minerals above it. Me, you, we are the minerals, we are the value of this land.

The red, yes it's blood but not just blood but passionate blood.

It is the will to survive, the resolve to carry on, it is the want to push through to see the dreams come to pass.

This Flag.

The black, the black is the night sky.

That which we emerge from and we shine.

It is the brilliant colors, it is the wonderful and lovely fruition of everything that we have ever hoped for. It needs a black for it to be visible.

This flag.

It is my country.

My Zimbabwe, we go through so much, we don't look like much even now but there is promise in it.

I will fight for it, I will live for it and I will stand for it.

This is the time...

That a change must happen. Quit standing on the sidelines and watching this flag fly and wishing for a future that you are not at all wanting to get involved in.

This flag, every day that it flies it is begging for you to get involved.

It is begging for you to say something, it is begging for you to cry out and to say, must we be in the situation that we are in?

This flag.

It is your flag.

It is my flag.

This flag.

. . .

I remember watching that for the first time and feeling the power of his words through my computer screen. My heart was moved by this man that had given me countless rides home from the youth group he pastored on Friday nights. I knew him, but the man on the screen was almost unrecognizable. He was a giant. He was a man among men. As he signed off I thought this must have been what it felt like when you were given a speech before going into an ancient battle. The only difference was this: there was only one man in that video. And if what we had grown up knowing of the Zimbabwean government was true, he had hours— at best, days—before disappearing, never to be seen again. The hunted had become the hunters and they were ruthlessly unapologetic about it.

The video went viral in Zimbabwe and across the globe. Major networks in the region were playing it on their news cycles hourly until international networks started to pick it up. No one had ever stood up to Mugabe and his croons. No one would ever dare do it publicly either. Unless maybe you had a powerful army backing you somewhere in the world or you were just a crazy pastor. I would like to think that the Zimbabwean government wasn't going to call Evan's bluff. They must have thought, surely someone greater is behind this. Maybe it was the nature of his video being so public. Maybe it was how quickly it went viral that slowed them down. But with each day he was free, Zimbabweans found a new champion, and through one man's bravery we too had found our voice.

Day after day Zimbabweans near and far watched as their fearless pastor continued to make videos confronting the brokenness he saw around him. Each time he made a video he would make it clear that he was just an ordinary Zimbabwean citizen who wanted a better Zimbabwe. For all his efforts, those in power remained silent. Then it was a few weeks after the first video that Pastor Evan called for all Zimbabweans to protest by staying away from work. See it is illegal to gather in groups of more than eight people and demonstrate on the streets in Zimbabwe. So this stay-away was a legal form of protest. The response would show the government just how many people were dissatisfied with the state of events in the country. The day came for the non-protest protest and about nine million Zimbabweans stayed at home. If Evan didn't have the government's attention before, he certainly had it now!

It wasn't long before he was arrested and placed in cuffs and sent to jail. I feel like in his time in jail the country was holding its breath just waiting to hear what we all were sure was the inevitable, that our hero pastor had fallen ill in prison and died or some other made-up story. While we waited, citizens both near and far started changing their profile pictures to "free Pastor Evan" images and the longer he was in prison the louder the voices got. It was on the day of his appearance before a judge that the nation really took a turn it had never taken in thirty-six years. It was at the Magistrates Court where Pastor Evan was scheduled to go where thousands of Zimbabweans gathered outside, a crowd making sure the government knew they had his back. Zimbabweans were never like this. They had been intimidated for so long that surely they didn't have any boldness left in them. But they were wrong. We did! I say "we" because even though I wasn't there everything in me wanted to be. I watched Facebook that day with the same zoned-out intensity that a teenager has when they're playing Fortnight or Minecraft. I sang with the crowds as the videos emerged, I prayed and I wept with my wife. They charged him with threatening to subvert a constitutionally elected government and this charge carried with it a maximum twenty-year sentence. These were the same charges brought against Mandela in South Africa and against Mugabe by the Rhodesians. Pastor Evan was now in revolutionary company.

The singing of hymns and worship songs outside the courthouse got louder and the crowd's prayers were so loud that the judge had to send people from within the courtroom to ask for silence because he couldn't hear the lawyers' arguments. Fifty human rights lawyers stepped up to defend Pastor Evan! It was epic! The images from that day will forever be etched in my memory as the day Zimbabwe stood up for itself. As darkness fell, the crowds did not leave but rather people went home to get blankets and candles to show they were not going anywhere without our pastor: a sign of defiance that had never been seen by this government. At about 7pm local time the judge did the unthinkable. He did only what could have been accomplished by the Spirit of God. He threw the case out and declared that the State had no case, thus making Evan Mawarire a free man. As he walked out the crowds cheered his name and he addressed them like he had been a statesman for decades. If ever there was a time I could say this man was born for this, it was then. Looking at him give his speech in front of journalists and a jubilant crowd of black, white, indian, mixed race... I mean you name it, they were there. A united Zimbabwe—finally.

At the moment Pastor E, as I call him, would have been told that there was credible intel that his life would be taken that night and that they would have to sneak him out the country immediately if he was to live. Just like that, a movement had been birthed and Mugabe's *Jumping the Shark* episode began. I figure someday Pastor E will write a book so I better stop there. My point is this: there he was, an ordinary patriot who practiced his patriotism, and it reignited a love for their country in millions of Zimbabweans who had lost it.

That was Nehemiah's call: to restore, rebuild and bring back pride where there was shame. That is what patriots do. I also know that not everyone reading this is from Zimbabwe, but I ask you put on the goggles of your nation and see what patriotism looks like. If Pastor E had been a nationalist he would have cast the blame on the state o the nation, on the foreigners and the outsiders. Instead he rallied people around restoration of Zimbabwe without oppressing anyone in the process.

When nationalism turns into xenophobia.

I have observed nationalism closely, and by nationalism I mean the dictionary definition and not your favorite news channel's definition of it. I see there is an inevitability that is birthed from it and that strong belief in the superiority of a nation starts to aim its anger toward immigrants. There starts to be a rhetoric that places the blame of everything that is going wrong on foreigners and immigrants. In the world of nationalism, not all immigrants are created equal. For example, I was talking to someone the other day and I dared to refer to myself as an expat. The look on their face was one of utter shock and the cat that got their tongue was a freakin' lion! I mean why not? I absolutely fit the description, I told myself.

Expat is short for "expatriate". Its simple definition is someone who lives in a foreign country. That's me, right? Wrong. Expat is often used to define white Westerners who live in a foreign country and everyone else is referred to as an immigrant. Now granted, there are people who refer to some white people as immigrants in almost every country all over the world, but the term expat is never reserved for someone who isn't white. So when nationalism rears its ugly head it's normally pointed at the non-white community. I don't say this at all to point my finger at any particular nation but it is in Africa where I have actually seen nationalism rear its ugly head and switch gears to xenophobia. Xenophobia, if you have never heard of the word, means a deep-rooted fear toward foreigners. South Africa is the one country that comes to mind. Xenophobic attacks seem to sprout every few years and there are a number of causes. Here are some of them:

• South African exceptionalism, or a feeling of superiority in relation to other Africans.

• Relative deprivation, specifically related to competition in the job market.

• Dangerous group-think, including psychological catego-rizations that are nationalistic.

• Exclusive citizenship, a form of nationalism that excludes others.

These are just a few of the causes that have cost many lives over the last decade. When observing xenophobic attacks in South Africa in 2015, my heart was extremely troubled. I watched as a whole community stood by, cheering as a man was being set alight in the middle of a street, in what they call "necklacing". Necklacing is when they beat you and drag you into the streets, then put a rubber tire over you, douse you with petrol, and set you on fire. These gruesome scenes flooded our newsfeeds on social media but the most shocking part was seeing all the onlookers condoning these acts. All this just because this man was a foreigner with a successful business in the community.

It was during an interview with one of the onlookers that a journalist asked why they did this. He said they did it because all the foreigners took away their jobs and must leave South Africa. He was quoting the Zulu king who sparked this wave of attacks in a speech addressed at a rally earlier that year. The journalist who was white and British, and also happened to be part of the 300,000 British nationals that live in South Africa, asked this follow up question—"What about me? I'm a foreigner, should I leave too?" The man, caught a little off guard, responded with what I believe is the darkest reality of all of our history as Africans. He simply said, "Not foreigners like you." Apartheid and the world around him taught him to hate his fellow African brother and never regard a British national as a foreigner. That man was making the distinction between immigrants and expats without even knowing it. Immigrants could be burned alive in the streets but expats were not to be touched.

Can you imagine what the news would look like if a caucasian British man was burned alive in an African street? Can you imagine the hashtags and the Union Jack profile picture changes? He was right—expatriates should never be touched, or you'll face dire consequences.

Nationalism has racism embedded in it and it can lie dormant for a while but it awaits to fully bloom when economic pressure hits a nation. No one would ever imagine that at some point they could stand in the streets watching their neighbor burn, but it happens. It happens slowly, but it happens. When a loss of money and an economic downturn is involved, the intensity goes up significantly. The destruction that follows is just a byproduct of the master called money. I believe this is why the Bible denounces nationalism so strongly throughout and reminds us to be mindful of the foreigner.

> "When a stranger sojourns with you in your land, you shall not do him wrong. You shall treat the stranger who sojourns with you as the native among you, and you shall love him as yourself, for you were strangers in the land of Egypt: I am the Lord your God. (Leviticus 19:33-34.)

> There is neither Jew nor Greek, there is neither slave nor free, there is no male and female, for you are all one in Christ Jesus. (Galatians 3:28.)

> But you are a chosen race, a royal priesthood, a holy nation, a people for his own possession, that you may proclaim the excellencies of him who called you out of darkness into his marvelous light. (1 Peter 2:9.)

THE HYPE

We are all looking for a tribe. Let's just get that out the way. We want something to belong to—a cause worth fighting for. Some are content to find this tribe in a knitting club, some find it in a gang, and some find it in an ideology that's all about the superiority of their nation. Unity in and of itself can be a very beautiful thing but it can also be very ugly depending on what you are uniting around. If you are uniting around the beauty of a nation and the amazing place that it has been to everyone, then it is awesome. If you are uniting on the negative aspects of why things aren't working or your disdain for something, then it is ugly. The hype of the latter is we start to become a clique that is not welcoming to everyone, and those who are not part of us become the "others". We are now united in our brokenness and our weapons are aimed at what we hate rather than what we love.

I keep saying over and over again in this book that hype has a shelf life. It moves on to something else or you have to up the ante for it to be maintained. It no longer becomes enough to just hate others, it turns into how to get rid of them completely—even off the face of the earth. When we look at history we see that there are people we absolutely disdain that allowed nationalism to live to its fullest hype and almost destroyed the whole world in the process. I read these words by President George W. Bush and I feel like they apply to many in the U.S and around the world:

"We've seen nationalism distorted into nativism – forgotten the dynamism that immigration has always brought to America. We see a fading confidence in the value of free markets and international trade – forgetting that conflict, instability, and poverty follow in the wake of protectionism."

When we buy into the hype of nationalism we dishonor God by forfeiting our opportunity to gladly take the gospel to every nation and tongue, with joy in our hearts. We lose out on a richer future not only for ourselves but for our children too. As for the Church, well it's obvious that there is no place for nationalism, as it's defined by the dictionary. There is only room for patriots. Patriots who move when asked to move and at the drop of a hat can adopt other nations in order to reach people with the gospel. To preach the gospel is our number one priority and our hearts should be set on reaching anyone, regardless of nationality.

The beauty of immigration is that it has brought people from many oppressive nations that don't allow the gospel to be preached freely right to our doorstep. What will they be met with? Love or fear? It doesn't matter where you are in the world, when you get the chance to engage with people from other places you are being given the chance to love your neighbor. Hype will make you miss out on this beautiful opportunity.

THE HOPE

The whole story of the gospel is one of a God who came to open the door for the outsider. When we read the Bible as gentile Christians we should always open it knowing that the only reason we can do so is because Jesus made a way for the outsiders! The Bible is a book that shouts from heaven and echoes below: *The outsiders are in!*

It was around Christmas of 2018 when the immigrant caravan was heading for the U.S./Mexico border and the story of the birth of Jesus started to become more real than I had ever thought possible. Here on my screen was a story playing out of a husband and wife fleeing tyranny with their little child, as Herod went on a murderous rampage. We sang carols about this very thing happening to the Jesus we worship, as we sat in our warmth, celebrating the love of our Savior. Some who would say that Jesus is their Lord and master were burning with rage and consumed with fear over what would happen if all "those people" entered their country.

My heart immediately felt the worst as I heard people who worked in foreign countries that have become dysfunctional make a case as to why the caravan should be stopped from entering. I wasn't so stubborn as to not totally get where many people were coming from and how they could view this kind of compassion as unsustainable. I understand! But I also couldn't justify unsustainable compassion as a legitimate reason to not help someone in light of my own story, in light of the gospel, and seeing children standing outside desperate for our help. Not when we know Jesus and not when we have been transformed by His love.

My mind rushed back to what I saw happen in 2015 in South Africa. This may not have been the equivalent of a community watching a man burning in the middle of the street, but it was still ignoring the desperate cries of people in need. While we complained about how we didn't have enough resources to help, we showered ourselves with thousands of dollars in clothing and gadgets and even more in food that would eventually be thrown out. I couldn't help but see a Pastor Evan that was trying to flee a government trying to kill him and his family and being told at the border, "Sorry, entry denied."

These thoughts cross my mind when I re-read the story of the birth of Christ. What if Egypt had closed off their borders during that time? I imagine Mary and Joseph may not have been the only refugees making a run out of Bethlehem. What if the surrounding nations had done what we do today? And by "we" I don't just mean America or South Africa, I mean most nations that are better off than their suffering neighbors. What if Jesus had done that to us? What if He said, "Heaven is full. No more room here!"

Listen, I get it. It isn't simple to just open the floodgates and let people into a nation just because theirs is messed up. I totally get that. But having been on the other side of desperately needing help, I can empathize. Empathy is such an important thing to have for one another, especially when we don't quite know what it's like to walk in their shoes. My heart in all this is for us to take these things to God with hearts that truly feel for those in a desperate place. Empathy is all I ask us to have.

I'm so thankful that the message of the cross is one that says, "I will make a way for you. All of you." I'll end with this passage.

> 34 Then Peter began to speak: "I now realize how true it is that God does not show favoritism 35 but accepts from every nation the one who fears him and does what is right. 36 You know the message God sent to the people of Israel, announcing the good news of peace through Jesus Christ, who is Lord of all. (Acts 10:34-36.)

This is our great hope. God welcomed us all in, and no nation is above any other in His sight. He made us, and makes us into, one nation, one race in Him through Christ. Let us find it in our hearts to treat each other as people who can't ignore the will of His Word.

9

RACE

I used to be a racist.

As a black man, I feel like it is so much easier for me to talk about my racist tendencies than it is for my fairer skinned counterparts. One thing about my past racism was this—it was a racism that had a green light. It was socially acceptable based on who I was and the history of my ancestors and forefathers. I was actually allowed to be racist almost as a form of revenge on history. Of course, like with everything that wants to destroy your soul, I wouldn't have said that my behavior was racist. Oh no, by no means would I ever call that shovel a shovel. No, I had a more sophisticated name for my racism and it was interchangeable depending on the room I found myself in. I had more name changes than Prince or The Artist Formerly Known As, or—you get my point.

Oh—it also had a green light due to the fact that I was married to a white person. I mean, can you possibly have racism in your heart and marry someone of another race? The short answer is yes. I'm living proof of it. I may have categorized what was in my heart as a light form of racism but it was still present. Which means it is totally possible for you to be racist and adopt a child from another country, or to really like your boss of a different race and be racist; and yes it is very possible to harbor racism in your heart and have a best friend in high school who happened to have skin that was different from yours. The bar for racism is actually a pretty low one and whether you are discriminating based on your superiority or inferiority, you are still discriminating. We tend to categorize racism as the KKK or Black Nationalists but I've found it to have a broader market.

I first realized my own prejudice when my wife and I went to watch her little brother play rugby. It was a rugby match between Old Georgians, which is predominantly white, versus Old Hararians, which is predominantly black. I left the house excited to see my brother-in-law play that day for the Old Georgians. He has always been one of the top rugby players in Zimbabwe and this would be the first time I would get to see this young phenom play in years. As we got to the game we were running a little late and it had already kicked off. My eyes began to notice something right away. I noticed that the stands of supporters were divided along racial lines. All the Old Georgian supporters were white and the Old Hararians supporters were all black. It didn't take long for me to start to root inwardly for the team that was opposing my brother-in-law. I actually wanted him to lose the game. I had this weird feeling of wanting him to do well but in a losing effort, if you know what I mean. That game had ceased being about my brother-in-law and had become about "the blacks" versus "the whites".

As it went on, this game began to become something bigger for me than just a game. It began to represent every racist thing a white person had ever done to me. It represented every time I was told I wasn't invited to something because there were no black people invited. It represented my English-speaking primary school headmaster telling the black kids to stop talking in Shona while the Afrikaans-speaking white kids were allowed to speak in their language. It represented a moment as a teenager, having a dear friend telling me that we could no longer be friends because her friends didn't like the fact that I was black. It was a reminder of every image I saw on the television growing up of white policemen with dogs chasing down people who looked like me.

It was all of those things and it was also just a rugby match on a Saturday afternoon between two teams in a league. Was this racist? What would you call that—rooting against my own family just because the backdrop of the match seemed to represent more than it should? As much as I tried, I couldn't shake off my thoughts. Why was Old Georgians whiter than any other team in the league? They had to have something embedded in their recruitment system that kept it that way, right? Why didn't they have some level of equality at their club, thirty years after Zimbabwe's independence? These are all questions that drove the motives of my heart. Was I right to question everything that may have been at the root of the scene that was before me? Absolutely! But was I wrong not to root for my brother who wasn't racist at all and loved me like his very own flesh and blood from the moment we first met?

Every single thing I was going through that day was driven entirely by hurt. I wasn't anywhere near healed, let alone whole. It almost seemed that it didn't matter what white people would do to heal this hurt, my wife included. Nothing would heal it. As long as I knew that there were still white people somewhere out there that were unrepentant of their destructive history it wasn't going to be okay. I was finding a part of my identity in my hurt and I was never going to be free from it unless I started seeking God on how to be free. I obviously can't control the heart of an entire race of people but I can control the direction of my own heart. My attitude toward another race wasn't any less racist because I could justify it, but rather it was wrong if it went against the heart of God.

Racism is powerful because it is the identity we can see from a mile away. People treat us differently because of the stereotypes that have existed for generations before we even arrived on the scene. Out of all the identities I have spoken about in this book, I know this one is the one that has sparked wars, that has seen millions perish, and hidden darknesses have been unearthed. This one is close to home for me because even though I said I used to be racist, I still think we all have a little racism in us at some level. We have all made decisions to attend something based on whether more of "our kind" will be present, carried a fear toward another ethnicity, or have been silent in the face of racist behavior. We're all guilty. We just conceal our racism, therefore it is never healed.

WHY IT HURTS

I don't remember the first time I noticed I was black but I certainly remember the last time I was reminded that I am. Right at this very moment I am sitting in a coffee shop writing this book and as I gaze around I notice that I am the only black person in the room. I live in a place where I can feel out of place at almost every turn and I can't fully explain it in words but it's just something you feel. If you have ever felt unwelcome somewhere you know what this feels like. You're the most visible and the most invisible at the very same time. It is a weird feeling. In my neighborhood I am a very rare sight and people seem to live there when they "make it", which means it is largely Caucasian. No kidding! it is ninety-nine percent white. In my neighborhood I feel like white people should walk around saying, "If you're having race issues I feel bad for you son! got ninety-nine problems but being white ain't one!"

For example, this morning I was pulled over for the very first time in America. I had no clue why I was pulled over, because as I passed the police officer I made sure was going just under the speed limit (and by just under, I mean like six miles under). Okay maybe more like ten. I've learned something by watching all the headlines of all the shootings and that is you never know who is stopping you and what they are going to do when they get to your window. This is me just being real with you, so take it or leave it. All I could think about was the video I saw of Philando Castile, an unarmed black man, who was shot at a traffic stop just like the one I was now at. Now I know without a shadow of a doubt that most cops don't do that and they're not waking up in the morning trying to shoot someone just because they're black, but I had seen it happen way too many times to not have some level of fear.

I thought of how unfair it would be to my wife and daughters. No more daddy, just because he looked a certain way. I thought of being a post on people's Facebook pages, being the right bad news at the right, wrong time. I thought about what I think of when I see people attach their political arguments to somebody else's real life pain, basically using the death of a person and the pain of a family to tell their political adversaries "I told you so." I also thought of the silence. The ones who wouldn't say a thing because this tragedy doesn't fit their political views. Even though they personally knew me, they couldn't even address how this was an issue due to how it would actually affirm what they have been saying isn't happening. I honestly thought of all the thoughts and prayer posts that would pop up and all the wrong we have done in the wake of the deaths of many minorities who have been shot unjustly. I really did think about what it would really mean to people. This fear had been a result of images being thrown at me that were true but were also disproportionate. No one has been shot where I live and the policemen and women I know are in no way anything like that. This fear was embedded in me through my consumption of information that amplified the narrative.

Disproportionate images change how we think about every situation, but with some things, like people being shot, it doesn't matter how infrequent they occur. The fact that they even occur is the problem. If we saw an image every three months of a plane crashing it would affect the entire airline industry badly. People can see a car accident every week and we'd all still get into our cars and drive around, but the planes would change how I roll. If it was three crashes from one airline carrier that would almost definitely mean the end of their business. Some images, though disproportionate, are more of an issue due to what the images are. So when you see a cop shooting an unarmed black man during a routine traffic stop, you can't help but feel that it may happen to you too.

Now if you're thinking to yourself, "Rob, you have no right saying this," or maybe you're thinking, "Go back to Zimbabwe if you're so scared of the cops! These are the same guys who keep you safe and risk their lives to save you without you even knowing it!" I get it and I know why you would say that, I really do. If you are saying these things, I don't mean to stereotype you but you're probably white and you have never felt what I just expressed. O maybe you have. Maybe the one time you were walking alone on the one side of the street in a "bad part of town" two black men in baggy jeans, a hoodie and Timberlands were walking toward you and you switched over to the other side of the street. I mean you knew that chances were high that they're weren't going to do anything to you but maybe you watched *The Wire* and you saw how Stringer and Avon rolled. They fit every profile you have seen on your news station for decades and you have a little fear in you too. I have been the black guy on the side of the street in a good part of town, and have wondered why the poor ladies felt like they had to switch sides to avoid me. I am the most harmless person out there! I mean I was wearing the "international I am not dangerous" outfit... a Vineyard Vines polo and colorful Sperry's! Images that get thrown our way can absolutely affect how we treat one another and can embed a fear for another ethnicity deep in our hearts.

WHAT DOES GOD SAY ABOUT RACE?

More than anything else I have mentioned on this topic, the thing that hurts the most is silence. Silence hurts because it suggests someone doesn't care. The Bible says a few things about race but I believe, for the Christian, the Bible is very clear about those that follow Jesus being intentional about standing up for the oppressed.

> 3 Defend the weak and the fatherless;
> uphold the cause of the poor and the oppressed.

4 Rescue the weak and the needy;

deliver them from the hand of the wicked. (Psalm 82:3-4.)

I feel we have to start by establishing the heart of God when it comes to those who are being oppressed. We have to defend them and uphold their cause. The Bible is very clear about that! What does that look like in real life and not Bible life? Well, I guess you have to start with what defending someone looks like. Defending someone is definitely an action. I think it means speaking up when something happens to someone who is oppressed. Silence is never defense. *Never ever.* If I was scolded by someone for no reason and you were silent there is absolutely no way you can say after the fact that you defended me. We are so polarized today, more than ever, and I'm not just talking about my community here in the U.S. but in Zimbabwe as well. We have learned to take on the stances our political leaders take and have abandoned standing first and foremost on God's Word.

14 For he himself is our peace, who has made the two groups one and has destroyed the barrier, the dividing wall of hostility, 15 by setting aside in his flesh the law with its commands and regulations. His purpose was to create in himself one new humanity out of the two, thus making peace, 16 and in one body to reconcile both of them to God through the cross, by which he put to death their hostility. 17 He came and preached peace to

you who were far away and peace to those who were near. 18 For through him we both have access to the Father by one Spirit.

19 Consequently, you are no longer foreigners and strangers, but fellow citizens with God's people and also members of his household, 20 built on the foundation of the apostles and prophets, with Christ Jesus himself as the chief cornerstone. 21 In him the whole building is joined together and rises to become a holy temple in the Lord. 22 And in him you too are being built together to become a dwelling in which God lives by his Spirit. (Ephesians 2:14-22.)

God's Word tells us here in this passage that Jesus is our peace and that we are now one in Him. That the walls that divide us are gone if we are in Christ. Both Jew and Gentile now have access to worship together as one, and the foundation of this unity is Jesus. We are no longer foreigners or strangers but we are now fam. *We are one.* This is what the cross of Jesus did for us and we ought to honor that with everything we are. Church shouldn't be divided along racial lines, and diversity should be found more in a place of worship than in any other. There should be more unity in a church than at an arena full of people cheering for ten guys trying to put a ball in a hoop. But there isn't. Sunday is still one of the most segregated times of the week in America and, dare I say, the world. Can you imagine that on the day where we worship Jesus that says, "I died for you to be one," we still choose to be divided?

NOVEMBER 2016

The lead up to this date changed the community I call home and flipped it on its head. People who had seen eye to eye were now more divided than ever. They didn't even want to see each other let alone talk to one another. The presidential election had been so polarizing that for the first time people were all too willing to throw away relationships for the sake of some politician chasing their own ambitions. Not being American, I didn't have the ability to vote, so I didn't actually have a horse in the race. I was an observer of my very first election. I saw Christians reveal their first identity not as Christ but as a color. Red and Blue were greater than Jesus. Even though they would say it was in the name of Jesus they supported their colors, I saw through that. It was in the name of identity, fear, past hurts and self preservation. It was on all sides—people embracing a political identity with a sparse sprinkling of Jesus. But what followed honestly surprised me. There was pure hate and disdain for one another. There seemed to be nothing united about the United States of America. I thought to myself, I'm a novice, so I don't fully grasp American politics—and I honestly still don't. What I do grasp though, is a knowledge of God's Word and people's hearts. These seemed to be out of sync during that time. People surprised each other by exposing the hills they were actually willing to die on and in all honesty nothing has been the same since. Jesus died to make us one, yet we were so willing to let that go for so little.

I had the privilege of meeting a guy who worked for a congressman a few months ago and I asked him what was the wildest thing he observed while working in Washington. He told me how the politicians from opposite sides were actually friends after the cameras were switched off and the media cleared out. He mentioned how they have dinner with each other, play golf and even vacation with their contemporaries. I couldn't believe it! You mean to tell me there are families fighting each other over the things that politicians disagree on in public yet the politicians themselves have good relationships and hang out with each other at the club? It was almost like finding out that we were fighting each other over the things Hulk Hogan and Macho Man Randy Savage said on WWE, when in real life the dudes are like, it's just my job to fight. It's not real! We start saying things to one another that these politicians would never say to one another without apologizing.

WHEN RACISM WHACKS YOU IN THE FACE

A few years ago I experienced the boil over of this first hand when I was attempting to get my drivers license in a neighboring town. Now I've mentioned before that my wife is white, so in some situations it is easy for me to know we are being treated differently because of that. It was at this one particular DMV where I experienced the most blatant racial discrimination I've ever experienced living in the U.S. As I went to the counter, the man behind the desk asked me for my paperwork and after I handed it over to him he noticed I was an immigrant.

"What the F*** is this?" he asked.

I was taken aback. I didn't know someone could say that to you while serving you in America. Not only was it unprofessional but what the heck, man?

"It's my paperwork, sir," I replied. "I came here on a medical emergency and that's why it's probably not familiar to you."

Something in me told me this guy knows that you are at his mercy so you better act accordingly. He knows he controls whether or not you can get around and there is nothing you can do about it.

He looked down and then looked up at me and said, "So it's *my* taxes that are f***king paying for *your* medical bills!"

I was so shocked! I had just seen my wife go before me with the same papers and for her it was a breeze. Why was he doing this to me? He then intentionally forgot to put my number in the system so that I couldn't move on to the next phase of the process. It was after half an hour of waiting and seeing many others that were behind me get processed that it dawned on me. I asked a different person to help me and they reluctantly put me in the system. After my number was called I moved on to get my photo taken and that is when I knew that he really meant something by what he said. The lady taking my photo looked at me and said under her breath, "Don't worry, it's not everyone here that doesn't want people like you around. I'm glad you'r here." Until that point I could have written it off as a bad DMV experience but after that I knew what it was.

Wow! There are people that really don't want me around? That's wild! I got to the car and my wife asked me what took so long. I told her the whole story and like a glass filling up with raspberry Kool-Aid I could see her turning red with rage.

"I'm going in there right now!"

I told her to chill out. I told her there was no way a guy would say the things he said without knowing nothing can really happen to him. His manager was just like him and they would just delay my licensing process longer if I even dared. I just wanted it to be behind me, to be honest. My wife and I were both immigrants who were at the mercy of a man who assumed that he was paying my bills. A narrative that was completely untrue in my case but depending on what news channel you watched it was one that was being disproportionately projected daily. How I wished I had been there with my American friend, Lu. Pardon my example but she would have ripped him a new one and demanded that he be fired for such appalling behavior. She would have spoken up for me. I know that because she embodies every part of the passage of Scripture above. That's also why I didn't tell her. I didn't want drama. I just wanted to drive again.

Our silence is often driven by our lack of understanding what it feels like to be in a situation like this one I found myself in. If you have never been in a situation where you've been treated unfairly due to the color of your skin, which was obvious in my case due to my wife having her case heard with no ill words spoken, you tend to minimize the severity of the hurt afflicted. You minimize my experience based on your own experiences. You make excuses like he was just a rude man and none of it was based on my appearance at all. You think of your own experience at the DMV or at something else where someone told you to F-off and you argue that it happens to everyone. You don't consider how I may have compounded all the images of the shootings and this man's discrimination into one file that came to mind when I got pulled over. That thing that stops us from seeing someone else's experience as legit... that thing is privilege. It is an absolute privilege to never have to experience something negative when others experience it regularly.

WHITE ADVANTAGE

Just the mention of the word "privilege" causes some people I know to tense up and get defensive. They automatically assume the word or phrase means you didn't work hard to have what you have. So let's clear that up before I go deeper.

It's simply not true. If that's what we hear when we hear the term "white privilege" then of course I get why there is defensiveness, but this is a shallow definition of the term. So let's for the sake of this part call it an "advantage". White advantage. Sometimes when I look at the history of the world, including the part of the world I'm from, I think to myself how it is possible to be white and not think there is some level of advantage attached to your whiteness? Every time a white person says I don't have an advantage based on my skin color it always sounds a little Lance Armstrongish to me. I think of what they're really saying deep down inside. They're saying, "I didn't have an advantage where I grew up, around my peers who also happened to be white." In your neighborhood it was a level playing field. I get that. You may have even been at the bottom of that pile too, which is why your blood boils when someone suggests you didn't work hard for what you have. But, oh yes, there is a but...

The best way for me to describe advantage is through the lens of the life of Lance Armstrong. Lance Armstrong's story first came to global notoriety when he beat Stage 3 testicular cancer, which had spread to his lungs and brain. He beat that! He underwent chemotherapy and multiple surgeries and in 1999 rose to win the greatest race in the world of cycling, the Tour de France. He would go on to win this race seven freakin' years in a row! Let that settle in your spirit. Seven! He then established Livestrong, an organization helping cancer patients globally, which became a movement which would generate over $470 million. Nike sold $100 million worth of the yellow Livestrong wristbands. About 225,700 people were served by the organization and $85 million worth of grants were given away. I'm not even considering the amount of revenue the sport of cycling generated in viewership and new interest during the Armstrong Tour de France run. He was an enigma, loved by all and representing hope to millions affected by this disease called cancer, a disease which Lance obliterated and sent packing like his cycling competitors. We were enamored, every single one of us, and if you weren't, you would have to root against a man who beat cancer. Impossible... you just couldn't.

I watched the Oprah interview when Lance Armstrong finally admitted he had lied. When he came clean about doping. He cried and said some of the right things but he just didn't look or sound very sorry. We all know what that looks like because we have all been "sorry, not sorry" before. We have all been caught at some stage in our lives and yet justified ourselves. It shows in our apology. He mentioned at one point that everyone was doping when he was winning. I mean the evidence is overwhelmingly true that everyone was doping during that time, and if you didn't dope no one would even remotely remember you today. Lance Armstrong had an advantage and so did almost everyone else, but he still had the advantage. I'm fighting really hard not to say that Lance was the dopest of the dopers.

Here is how this relates to privilege or advantage. Lance cheated but he also worked hard. He still had to cycle up the mountains and beat out other dopers. He had an advantage that he could justify by saying others had that same advantage, but that was absolutely unforgivable around those that didn't dope. Around those without his means, resources or privilege, for the sake of the point, he was untouchable. Even though the results of this advantage helped thousands and maybe even assisted in giving his accusers much needed publicity for the sport of cycling, it was still unfair and unjust. As unfair and unjust as it is though, Lance still genuinely beat cancer. He still gave away a real $85 million to those that really needed it. He still brought hope even if only for a season. It was much needed hope for the suffering.

Yes, you worked hard. Maybe in white suburban America your advantage wasn't really an advantage. Maybe it wasn't even the effects of slavery that gave you a leg up. Maybe you are second generation American and your family is originally from Europe so your benefits come from colonization. You, like my white wife, may not find your advantage in hundreds of years of free labor but maybe just in your whiteness at a DMV somewhere. I know this is an oversimplification of a very complex issue but I am trying to show you that a special advantage can exist alongside helping many—alongside hard work and even alongside helping those that accuse you or expose you. It exists in the midst of those things rather than those things nullifying the presence of privilege. So yes, maybe there were cyclists that didn't dope but also didn't work hard—it doesn't matter because Lance still had an unfair advantage over them.

What is privilege? I have been learning lately that I throw out a lot of words without really getting down to the actual definition of the word. Privilege, according to the Oxford dictionary, is a special right, advantage, or immunity granted or available to a particular person or people.

So when I look at that definition I find myself thinking, if there is a group of people less likely to have something happen to them based on the color of their skin, then they have the privilege to not experience that. It is no question that if you see images of young African American's being gunned down, unarmed, and also see images of white extremists murdering multiple innocent civilians with an automatic weapon and then being apprehended alive, with their dignity (what's left of it) intact, that is the presence of privilege in a society. It is hard to face this truth and I didn't know how hard it was until God showed me my own tribal privilege.

SHONA PRIVILEGE

In Zimbabwe, Shona's make up seventy percent of the population while the Ndebele's make up twenty percent. The last ten percent is split between other tribes and races. Shona's occupy most of the northern part of Zimbabwe with Ndebele's taking up the more southern part of the country. The two main cities in Zimbabwe are pretty much drawn along these tribal lines. Shona's live in Harare, the nation's capital, and the Ndebele in Bulawayo, the second largest city. My mom was a Shona who was raised in Bulawayo and till this day I'm not quite sure how that came about but it's just was how it was. My mom had two children before she married my dad and my half brother were Ndebele's. My cousins on my mom's side of the family also mainly resided in Bulawayo. Growing up, these differ ences never seemed weird to me. I never thought about why my cousins and my brothers could all speak my language, Shona, and yet I didn't speak a lick of Ndebele. They had to learn how to communicate with me but I didn't have to learn to communicate in their language. Why didn't my mom teach me her mother tongue when I was little? I may have thought that a couple of times growing up but no more than that. I had privilege and I didn't know it. I also didn't realize just how privileged I was being born a Shona. Despite the clear and obvious fact that I was in the majority tribe there was also an ugly elephant lurking in Zimbabwe's short history... *Gukurahundi*.

Nine months before I was born in January, 1983 a military attack named *Gukurahundi* (meaning "early rain that washes away the chaff") was launched by the North Korean trained 5th Brigade against the minority Ndebele's in the southern part of Zimbabwe. These attacks were by all means being carried out by the Shona government, trying to squash any type of uprising by the Ndebele's after independence. There is more history as to what led up to these attacks but to go into those would mean writing a whole book in itself. I hope this will be done extensively some day. Accounts of these atrocities are so vague and have been kept silent for so many years that it's hard to give accurate figures as to what transpired. What we do know is that around 20,000 Ndebele's were murdered in what the former Zimbabwean president Robert Mugabe has only been quoted as calling "a moment of madness."

My brothers grew up during that period in the southern part of the country and experienced some of this first hand. They saw and heard things that no child in their early teens should ever experience. Everyone knew what was happening in that part of the country but there was so much fear and intimidation at the time that everyone just remained silent. It may have been why so many of my Ndebele cousins could speak Shona so well. It may have been why my mom never taught me how to speak Ndebele —you didn't want to grow up being a potential target of the 5th Brigade. I've heard accounts of buses being stopped because suspected instigators were on board. These militants would line up the men and ask the women to dig shallow graves behind them. Then they would shoot the men and command the women to bury them. I can't imagine the pain of burying your son in the middle of nowhere after seeing him shot in cold blood. The grief, the anguish, and the anger toward the men who did this to your loved ones and yet no one to report to. Just crying in silence.

These attacks finally stopped after a unity accord was signed on December 22, 1987, between the Prime Minister Robert Mugabe, a Shona, and Joshua Nkomo, the Ndebele leader. Nkomo was given the post of vice-president and served in that position until his death in 1999. No one spoke about these atrocities publicly—ever. There wasn't a text book with any of that in it. There wasn't a single news report to be found. I only found out about what it was when I was in my twenties. I had the privilege to neve have to worry about it. Some of my relatives from the south though didn't have the same luxury. They grew up knowing what the Shonas were capable of. They grew up full of suspicion and the silence from my side must have been deafening.

Silence is a privilege. Facing ugly parts of history and repenting for them is one step in a long list of steps in the healing process. In my opinion, silence is no longer an option. I can't allow my privilege to somehow trick me into justifying not speaking up. I may not have ever said a bad word about a Ndebele or hurt one personally but people like me did. In my fight against others who have been on the side of the oppressor I must take a deep look at where I have been the oppressor myself. It is the hardest thing to do but Jesus tells us to take the log out of our own eye before we go about the business of taking the speck out another's.

Our logs are hard to see. That is why Jesus talks about it. My own privilege took years and years to even come up to the surface and it took even longer to repent of. Our own privilege is incredibly hard to spot. My kids being lighter-skinned have to be aware of theirs too. Bi-racial or lighter-skinned black people have a history of discrimination toward darker-skinned people. Some of the worst forms of discrimination that I have encountered in my life have been inflicted by people who are bi-racial. My kids are bi-racial and so I teach them to be aware of the advantage they have by virtue of being lighter-skinned and having a white parent. It changes what they are exposed to and really does give them a certain immunity in particular instances. Yet I have seen bi-racial people demanding white people listen to them about their struggle as a black person while ignoring their own specks. Colorism is a thing that affects the black community and representation in media has for a long time painted darker people, especially women, as being "less than". There is a call to restoration there too.

Specks and logs. There are enough of those to go around. But the thing we are *all* being called to is *humility*. We are being called to go out of our way to make it possible for those who may not be seen or heard to know that they are.

Now Jesus learned that the Pharisees had heard that he was gaining and baptizing more disciples than John— 2 although in fact it was not Jesus who baptized, but his disciples. 3 So he left Judea and went back once more to Galilee.

4 Now he had to go through Samaria. 5 So he came to a town in Samaria called Sychar, near the plot of ground Jacob had given to his son Joseph. 6 Jacob's well was there, and Jesus, tired as he was from the journey, sat down by the well. It was about noon.

7 When a Samaritan woman came to draw water, Jesus said to her, "Will you give me a drink?" 8 (His disciples had gone into the town to buy food.)

9 The Samaritan woman said to him, "You are a Jew and I am a Samaritan woman. How can you ask me for a

drink?" (For Jews do not associate with Samaritans.) (John 4:1-9.)

In this passage we see a story of a woman who was full of shame. She couldn't even muster up the courage to go to the well with other women, as was the custom at that time. She was hiding because she wasn't good enough. The blemishes of her past and present prevented her from having community. Jesus totally set her free with one lunch-time conversation. I mean this was an encounter that centered around water and created an on-fire evangelist! Can you imagine that? A Fiji water ministry bringing the promiscuous to repentance?

Among the many amazing things in this story you find there is one line that is incredibly powerful. Verse 4 says Jesus *had* to go through Samaria. The journey from Judea to Galilee was one that a good Jewish Rabbi would not take by going through Samaria. It wasn't the thing to do when one embarked on this journey. Until this day, this area, Samaria, which we know today as the West Bank, is still a conflict zone between Israel and Palestine. The reasons why Jews didn't pass through Samaria was because of the racial conflict that existed between the two groups, and this woman points this out in verse 9 by saying, "How can you ask me for a drink?" The Bible even tells us: (For Jews do not associate with Samaritans.) They couldn't even ask each other for a drink of water yet, and when we read, we notice that Jesus leads His disciples who would have known about this beef through this place. God cuts through the racism like a knife and forces not only His disciples to learn through this but the woman to be free from her personal shame.

This passage teaches us that we have to be present and in close proximity with those who don't look or act like us in order to experience healing. Jesus not only does that for this woman but later in that passage we see that many came to believe in Jesus because of her testimony. Sometimes the thing we are being asked to do is not some grandiose gesture or to start a movement that changes legislation but rather just go through a place and be present there. Sometimes it is just choosing to drink water in a place you have never drank water before—joining a gym in an area that looks different from yours—and it may mean you have to go a fair bit out of your way to do so. Sometimes it means joining a Bible study at another church or going to events in another community, sitting down with people and asking them what their journey looks like. Whatever it is, a little bit of going out of your way may change someone's life or perception of "your people." Maybe it's being proactive in making strangers feel welcome.

MANGWANANI

I remember walking into the Starbucks I frequent and seeing a new guy working there. He stood out mainly due to how the way he dressed and his cool looking hat made me notice him even more. There was something astro physicist about the look he had going on and yet he was a barista. As I got to the counter he greeted me with an incredibly chirpy but warm, "Hello, how can I help you?"

Now whenever I order a drink from Starbucks I usually draw some attention when I say "tall" and this occasion was no different. As I ordered my coffee he noticed my accent.

"Where you from?" he asked.

"I'm Zimbabwean".

"Oh—do you speak any other languages?" he asked.

"Yes."

"How do you say 'good morning' over there?"

"*Mangwanani.*"

He pulled out a pen and pad out of his back pocket and asked, "how do you spell that?"

As I was spelling it out for him I found myself way more intrigued than I had initially been. I wondered why this was so interesting to him. I spelled it out: "M-a-n-g-w-a-n-a-n-i."

It was on a wet winter morning months later that I needed this man the most. I was feeling so downcast. I wanted to be home and I was having one of those "no one here gets me" kinda days. It was on that day, when I felt most invisible, most unwelcome, when I walked into that Starbucks to get something to warm me up. Starbucks was packed, which didn't help raise my spirits either. As I walked in, slouchy and dreary, I heard the loudest "*MANGWANANI!*" pierce through the room! I smiled, looked up and said "*Mangwanani!*" right back to him. My heart warmed up again. After months of practicing this greeting, Jeff had it down, accent and all! I needed that! I needed to feel noticed but also embraced in a place where I normally just feel unnoticed. In my five years of being in that area no one had dared make me feel at home in that way. No one had attempted to even learn just the greeting in my language. I know, I know, people were probably afraid to risk trying it, then botching it, then being called racist! I say only as a joke! Still, this—this made me feel something. It changed my entire day. One pen, one notebook, and one intentional question.

Sometimes going out of our way isn't as big as we think. It takes intentionality to notice people who are different from us. Sometimes it takes listening over a glass of water or whatever beverage of choice. It's remembering how to say hello and perfecting just one thing to make people feel welcome.

God made all the races of humankind different and unique. Not so that we can find ways to separate ourselves and pretend that we don't see the difference, but rather to celebrate our diversity. To admire the creativity shown in His creation and therefore worship Him. Racism is a beast that won't just go away quietly. It's been around for way too long and has destroyed many lives over many centuries. I believe healing starts by revealing where we have been hurt and confessing and repenting to those we hurt. It starts by confronting our ugly history and having life-giving conversations with one another. It starts by saying, I have a rac problem and I want Jesus to pierce through that like He did with the woman at the well.

THE HYPE

TO THE WOKE,

I'm sitting in a coffee shop and I just saw a man walk up to my car and try to open it as I was writing this. As I watched, literally moments ago as he peeked in the back of the car, I wondered if this white middle-aged man was trying to break into my car. He's wearing sweats and those weird shoes with the slots for your toes that white people wear (very stereotypical of me, I know). I saw him wrestling with the door a little while holding his grande white chocolate mocha or whatever in the other hand. I can't believe this—I'm being robbed by a white guy while writing a chapter on race, and my name is Rob! The irony! Then I saw it hit him. That's not his car... he looks around and there it is! I see the light bulb switch happening with my own two eyes. He walks away from my car and over to his black Kia Silento or something that sounds like that and drives away. I thought to myself, not all black crossovers look the same bro. I mean it was his car and he mistook mine for his just because it was black. Then I thought again, what would I think If he mistook me for another black *guy*? What if he walked up to me and said that has been said to me a million times? Hi, Shalom! I hate that. I automatically think to myself that's the other black guy, racist! Sometimes people just make mistakes and sometimes people are bad with faces. I am one of those people! Not everything is racist but some things are. That is the tension. We all need discernment!

In the world we are living in we are being asked to view things through the lens of outrage. Everything is about division in the name of justice. Don't get me wrong, there is a need for justice and for there to be confession, repentance and true reconciliation. Black people and white people who live in places where racism or colonialism has a history should have a truth and reconciliation season. The wound needs to actually heal. But while I say that I also say this: not everything is racist. Some things are people just making mistakes. Some things are just a lack of enlightenment. If anger is our motivation I believe people will sense that and automatically run as far as they can from confronting the darkness of the past. We can talk about white fragility all we want but I honestly believe that in Christian community there is fragility everywhere and therefore if we can find it in ourselves we should handle with care in order to be healed. As black people or white people who "get it", the spiritual onus is on you to bridge the conversation with the heart of Christ.

I one hundred percent know that this is counter intuitive after centuries of oppression and not to mention everything we go through in today's world. We are going to hear inflammatory things, we are going to hear ignorant things, and maybe even outright racist things. But ou hearts have to be healing. We need to have hearts of reconciliation—not proving that we were wronged so that we can win an argument.

TO THE RACIST,

My prayer is that you first and foremost understand that there is no racism in Christ. Some reading this may think this is a no brainer but I have met people who believe that their lives have been transformed by Jesus and yet they are still incredibly racist. I had one of the most sincere conversations with a couple that told me in Zimbabwe that they were embarrassed to have dinner in public with an interracial couple from their church. My wife and I quickly realized why they insisted we come over to their place for dinner. That was probably one of the most unexpectedly racist and hurtful things that has happened to me. This thing called racism exists because it is never really confronted. How can you be growing in relationship with Jesus and still hold fast to that ideology? Then I realized this guy was confessing. He was not telling us this to brag or boast but to confess that his heart was broken and that it was ugly. There has to be room in our churches for confession and for the racist to be able to say, "this is the sin I struggle with." There needs to be room in church, or else all we will have are undercover racists who act like they don't struggle with that and are too ashamed to confess their brokenness.

I have met so many that have this sin and don't even

know it because they have convinced themselves that their racism isn't actually racism. If there are things that blatantly happen to another group of people that don't look like you and you are unwilling to speak up, then like me, with my Shona heritage, you have a privilege that allows you to be silent. If you are afraid to defend the weak due to fear of how your community would treat you then you have a racist community that you fear more than you fear God. If you see others as less than you due to the color of their skin or ethnicity then that is racism that needs to be confronted. Confront it, repent of it, and drink deeply of the grace God has afforded us through the cross of Christ.

I want to encourage you to read this and soak in this passage of scripture before moving on. Don't get defensive but allow God to wash over you with truth. No condemnation, just His love and grace. I pray His kindness leads us to repentance.

> 21 But now apart from the law the righteousness of God has been made known, to which the Law and the Prophets testify. 22 This righteousness is given through faith in Jesus Christ to all who believe. There is no difference between Jew and Gentile, 23 for all have sinned and fall short of the glory of God, 24 and all are justified freely by his grace through the redemption that came by Christ Jesus. 25 God presented Christ as a sacrifice of atonement, through the shedding of his blood—to be received by faith. He did this to

demonstrate his righteousness, because in his forbearance he had left the sins committed beforehand unpunished— 26 he did it to demonstrate his righteousness at the present time, so as to be just and the one who justifies those who have faith in Jesus. (Romans 3:21-26.)

There is no difference between Jew and Gentile. We have *all* sinned sinned and *all* fall short. It is the same grace poured on the thief on the cross, on the persecutor of those who followed Jesus, on the porn addict, that is the same grace poured on the racist. His grace is available.

THE HOPE

"Just preach the gospel". I have often heard this when discussing this issue. People normally say this as a cry to abandon talking about the sin of racism. It is a political issue that errs on the wrong side of the majority of the church in America and it is seen as a liberal argument because racism simply isn't as prevalent as it once was. Can you imagine that rationale applied to any other area of your life? Imagine hearing the school principal say to you that you should quit complaining because the school bully that used to punch your kid every day was now down to just punching them twice a week. What parent in their right mind who love their child would stand for that? Just because racism is "not as bad as it used to be" doesn't mean we shouldn't address it.

Racism is not a political issue but rather a gospel issue that has been politicized. So for all the Facebook posts that say just preach the gospel—should we do that with every issue? I actually don't entirely disagree with the notion "just preach the gospel". In fact, I believe the gospel speaks to all these issues if we actually just preach the actual gospel! If we just preached the gospel we would talk about money a lot! Jesus spoke about that a lot. Where I live, "just preach the gospel" and talking about possessions as much as Jesus did would thin out the churches. That's not always a bad thing in my opinion so I do believe we should just preach the gospel!

Jesus, also in the gospels, attacks the sin of racism. It is this very thing that caused many a Pharisee to want to kill Jesus. Making Samaritans heroes in His parables and exalting a gentile's faith as being the greatest faith he had seen would have been highly controversial at the time. All of this was highly offensive in the eyes of the religious elite because if Jesus were around our churches today he wouldn't be using people of different races as the heroes in His messages but rather He probably would use enemies of the state. Can you imagine the hate that would be pointed toward Jesus today if he made heroes out of the people we despise? We are "gospel-lite" when it comes to our ability to offend, compared to Jesus. The difference is that we are human, we do lean left or right, and denying that would be ludicrous. The gospel on the other hand is an equal opportunity offender and it has no allegiance to any political view. It will challenge abortion and immigration with n apologies because God doesn't conform to us but rather we conform to Him.

So when it comes to race and reconciliation I believe the church has to lead. We have to lay down our lives and preferences for the gospel to shine through. To be honest, in the majority tribe or race, this bar is normally set very low. For some a show of the gospel is abandoning preference and sitting under a pastor who doesn't look like us. Minorities do it all the time and I believe when the majority race or tribe does this, it is very powerful. For some it is as easy as making your home a space for reconciliation to happen by listening to people's journeys. Maybe host listening dinners or gatherings where minorities share their stories uninterrupted to a group of majority people. For some it is repenting publicly. Imagine if majority tribe pastors gathered and met together to do this whenever something happened to minorities. The leaders of the church actually leading the charge to defend the weak—that would be something. It doesn't matter how woke you are and what t-shirt you own, if you are not influencing your community to repent and build relationships with minorities, what are you doing? Consider becoming an active influencer in your community. We should be aware not to pollute our desire for justice with politics but rather center it entirely on Jesus. Entirely! We all have blind spots and we need to be aware of God's grace for us in our own areas while also having grace for others in theirs. We are now one race in Christ. We are one. We are one. We need to say that until we can walk it. We are one, we are new.

14 For Christ's love compels us, because we are convinced that one died for all, and therefore all died. 15 And he died for all, that those who live should no longer live for themselves but for him who died for them and was raised again.

16 So from now on we regard no one from a worldly point of view. Though we once regarded Christ in this way, we do so no longer. 17 Therefore, if anyone is in Christ, the new creation has come: The old has gone, the new is here! 18 All this is from God, who reconciled us to himself through Christ and gave us the ministry of reconciliation: 19 that God was reconciling the world to himself in Christ, not counting people's sins against them. And he has committed to us the message of reconciliation. (2 Corinthians 5:14-19.)

Jesus died for *all* so that we no longer view people from a worldly point of view. We see people through the lens of what Jesus has done and once they're in Christ we see them as *new*. Brand new! Our job as believers is to be reconcilers, not antagonists. Our mission is not to fight to be proven right but rather reconciling others to God through Christ. Jesus gave up His right to be right so that we could be made right with God, and this is the example we ought to follow.

Lastly, I believe the thing we are all called to is humility and repentance. God's kindness leads us to this. (Roman 2:4.) I am drawn to repent for my own privilege and my own blind spot. My ethnicity and my belonging to th

Shona tribe has brought some pain to my Ndebele brothers and sisters and I would ask with a heart that longs for reconciliation that you read my repentance below.

I want to take a moment in this book to repent to my brothers and sisters from the Ndebele tribe. I truly am sorry for the injustices you have faced in a land that is your own. I repent for the senseless deaths of those that were killed at the hands of people from my tribe. I have lived almost my entire life without even thinking about what it must feel like to live in a country where we, the Shonas, placed a ceiling of leadership over you, only ever allowing you to be second in charge. The gospel compels me to not only speak up but to prayerfully take up your cause, my brothers and sisters. This paragraph is not adequate and I know that there must be a constant posture of repentance and a desire for equal opportunity on our part as Shonas to restore what Gukurahundi *attempted to wash away. You were never chaff to be washed away but rather you were family to be protected. For that I am truly sorry. May you find it in you to grant me forgiveness in the name of Jesus Christ.*

CHURCH

Joshua Harris has left the faith. So have a bunch of people who were instrumental in my early life as a Christian, including a host of other pastors I've known over the years. Harris, the author of the book, *I Kissed Dating Goodbye,* kissed Jesus goodbye. But my heart isn't angered by that just because he wrote a book about purity twenty-two years ago. I pray for him—but to be honest not a whole lot. The people in my community need me to be a pastor for them, to walk alongside them and pray for them, and that's where my main focus has to lie. The guy who lives down the road from me, who used to love Jesus but has now left the faith as Harris has, needs me to be there for him. I live where I'm called to be and can't afford to get sucked into the celebrity pastor wave of today.

The church in America and the church in Zimbabwe loves to place men and women on pedestals that they were never meant to occupy. Pastors should never ever b celebrities. Like ever! But we line up around fifteen blocks, pay $199 to hear them speak, and buy the same five authors' books over and over again, because guess what? We love it! We can't wait for a celebrity to announce they follow Jesus and then line up a spot at our event for them to speak. Twenty-four year olds that can throw a perfect spiral into an end-zone are all of a sudden given every opportunity in every church to share their testimony about how they won a game because of Jesus. Really? Jesus helps people win games? There is absolutely no biblical, gospel-rooted grounding for that. Yet we buy it and we love it. We pass the mic to a famous twenty-four year old and never give it to the faithful twenty-four year olds that we know in our churches. We love the famous over the faithful. But as much as we love it, it was never the way Jesus intended it to be. Not church.

SO WHAT IS CHURCH?

The easy answer to this question is that church is a community of people who gather to live, learn and grow in Christ. But the more complex answer is a broader explanation found in the book of Acts. Before we do that, let me first share a story I heard a few months ago about a bakery. The Boudin Bakery to be more specific. This is a bakery with one of the most fascinating business success stories out there and is a big part of San Francisco's history.

I first heard about this bakery listening to a friend of mine preach a sermon that really drew me in. I wanted to know more about this bakery and how it started. Founded in 1849 by French immigrants right at the height of the San Francisco gold rush, this bakery stumbled upon something that would for ever change this city's culinary exploits. The reason why it is so famous is, wait for it... the dough! Not the dough that Jay-Z and Biggie were talking about when they said they love the dough but rather a special, incredibly valuable dough. *Lactobacillus sanfranciscensis* (you totally didn't say that right) is the special bacteria that makes San Francisco sourdough bread world-famous. The Boudin Bakery has a very special form of this bacteria, which is perfected by the indigenous yeast and the foggy climate. They love it so much that they even refer to it as the "mother". The mother dough, to be more precise.

Every single loaf of sourdough bread they make comes from this 160 year-old mother dough that has been carefully preserved from generation to generation. Without this dough, the bakery would cease to exist and the bread wouldn't have it's original tangy, addictive taste. It is kept under very tight supervision and carefully maintained each hour by well trained bakers. I mean when they transferred some of this dough from San Francisco to Sacramento they used a police escort to get it there. It is real how valuable this dough is.

The success of this bread is because of the presence of the original key ingredient. That is what the church has to be—a place that has the major, most valuable key ingredient present in all it does.

To find the mother dough of the church you have to

look at the book of Acts. In chapter two of Acts, we find the beginnings of what we now call the Church. It starts with 120 people gathered and Jesus saying adios as He is elevated into heaven. He's like, I'm out! It's been 33 years of being in this joint without indoor plumbing, I've done my deal. I saved y'all, now you gotta wait for the thing I promised you that is going to be better than having me around, which is the Holy Spirit. People are shocked as they look up in the sky with open mouths, like we all did when one of the main characters in *The Walking Dead* was suddenly killed off! You know which episode I'm talking about! So, Jesus is busy going and His disciples don't quite have the next play. When I read that I'm always like, "I love that this is God's MO (Modus Operandi) throughout the Word. He leaves us waiting on Him, relying on Him and Him alone for what's next." So two dudes dressed in white, looking fresh, ask everyone why they are looking up in the sky and remind them that Jesus is coming back the way He left. At that point everyone leaves the scene and heads upstairs somewhere, where they proceed to pick new leaders and Justus loses out to Mathias to replace Judas—who is now dead and also happens to be one of the points in Peter's compelling sermon.

Before you know it (probably after ten days), the room is overpowered by a sound so loud that the neighbors are drawn out to see what's going on. This powerful wind causes something to happen to the 120 people in that room and they start to speak in other peoples' languages. These bilingual people are now hearing their language being spoken and they are shocked at what is going on. "Tongues of fire" is what they all saw and the very first church service is getting creepier by the moment. Yes even creepier than the lady who brings her *shofar* to church and randomly blows it during worship! This is different though—no one panics and no one thinks it's creepy except the people outside. (Side note: When the Holy Spirit shows up it may get creepy, just explain what is going on and keep it moving.)

Back to Acts. They all know this is no doubt God at work. That is everyone except the onlookers. These guys assume everyone up there is drunk. Peter reminds them that the saying goes "it's 11am somewhere", not 9am... "we're not drunk—it's too early for that! this is God's work." Pause for a second with me. The beginning of Acts is wild! Can we just say that out loud together? This is wild. The beginning of the Church is wild! If this happened in your local church this Sunday at the 9am service you would freak out. The whole beginning of the formation of the Church defies logic. It is inexplicable power flowing through a room and it empowers a sermon that in turn sparks a movement. But what follows next is the crux of what I want to share in this chapter.

After Peter's sermon it says that people were "cut to the heart." That cut led them to ask an important question, which was, "What shall we do?" (Acts 2:37.) What shall we do? What an important question to ask after we have been cut to the heart. They were convicted and then wanted to act on their conviction. So Peter tells them to repent and be baptized. Note the simplicity of it all. Repent and be baptized! This is Church without denominations adding sugar and spice to it, just how Jesus intended. This right here, this is the mother dough of the church. Repent, be baptized and receive, and by this the Holy Spirit will be activated in you. Then Peter pleads with them to "leave this corrupt generation" which, translated today, would be the same as someone asking you to stop going with the flow. Jesus made Peter a fisher of men, of live fish not dead ones—because only dead fish go with the flow. And the church grew that day by three thousand!

The next day this group of people couldn't get enough and they were back. They went to work and came back to hear more. And through this, a community was being formed. It is in Acts 2:43-47 where we find just what life in this new community called Church was really like.

43 Everyone was filled with awe at the many wonders and signs performed by the apostles. 44 All the believers were together and had everything in common. 45 They sold property and possessions to give to anyone who had need. 46 Every day they continued to meet together in the temple courts. They broke bread in their homes and ate together with glad and sincere hearts, 47 praising God and enjoying the favor of all the people. And the Lord added to their number daily those who were being saved.

I really think today that most people don't leave Jesus

but rather they leave the Church. They leave organized religion and buildings and rigid schedules and building funds. They leave a place that looks like it's missing the thing it says it has. They leave the monotonous two fast songs, announcements, a little prayer, one slower song, a message, and then home. That system over time can feel like it lacks intimacy and relationship. It lacks life.

There are several things from the passage above that have strongly convicted me over the last few years, the main one being God's power and presence in the Church. I want to unpack these.

POWER WAS PRESENT

A few years ago while visiting friends in Southern California, we were out taking pictures of the sunset and enjoying our day when my (then) pregnant wife asked if we could find a bathroom urgently. Now I don't know about you but there are two things Starbucks can guarantee you: good coffee and a no-questions-asked clean bathroom. Gas stations could learn a thing or two about bathroom generosity from Starbs. So we drive around and find a Starbucks in a bougie part of town. My wife runs in and uses the restroom and on our way out a black SUV pulls up next to us. My friend Dan, who is a local, immediately says there is a famous person in that car. At first I wanted to drive away but my wife almost punched me in my chest and shouted, "If that's a celebrity, we're waiting to see who is!" We pause and ready ourselves like tourists in the

Serengeti waiting for a lion to pounce on a zebra. Seconds go by and nothing. Then the door opens and almost in slow motion, out comes a figure I easily recognize. Kobe "Freaking" Bryant!

We start going wild in the car! Except, of course, my almost four-year-old daughter in the back. She has no clue what has turned her family into screaming sugar-high five-year olds. Now at this point we realize that we must go back into the Starbucks and get a photo with him. I mean, I had never ever met a celebrity in my life and this was my chance! We devised a plan and bam! We decide to send in Dan and I with my daughter, leaving my wife to film the whole deal from the car. I go into the coffee shop and order the cheapest drink and wait. A few moments later Kobe walks in... and the Kobe aura is real, people. It's just us and the five-time NBA champion Kobe Bryant in that room. I look at him and he looks at me, and just like that... I choke. No words can come out of my mouth. The moment is gone as Kobe sits there waiting for his order. I can't believe I've blown my chance to get a photo with Kobe—that is until my daughter shouts at the top of her voice... "WHO IS KOBE?" Noooooooo! He now knows we know who he is! He knows why we're in that Starbucks! I can't quite quantify the embarrassment I feel but I see the chance to ask is now back on. I look at him and ask him if he doesn't mind getting a picture with my daughter because she's such a big fan. He says sure and as we set up to take the picture I make sure to hold my daughter far enough away from my body so that I can crop her out later! This is *my* moment girl!

Now there are a few reasons why I tell you that story.

We did a lot of adjusting to get into the presence of Kobe. We inconvenienced ourselves to encounter him. We waited patiently and we knew that if it worked out it would be worth it. His presence was worth pursuing without question. But, do we do that in our churches to be in God's presence? Do we inconvenience ourselves? Do we wait on the Lord? Do we spend money just to create an opportunity for that to happen?

My daughter didn't recognize whose presence we were in. We can also miss it. Everyone who knew who Kobe is was excited by the potential of being in his presence, but the one who didn't would have missed it. We can miss God's presence if we don't know what it looks like. We need to familiarize ourselves with what the presence of God is and what it's not. I knew what Kobe looked like even on a dark night. We should know what God's presence is like even when visibility is low.

After we got the selfie we didn't care too much for Kobe. We just wanted to meet him so that we had a good selfie to post and we missed out on asking questions that may have led to more. You get what you came for. We at times cheapen experiencing God to small takeaways and we miss the potential of deepening the relationship.

You must be thinking—okay Rob, all that from meeting Kobe? I know it's a bit much but that is how we are meant to be. That night Dan led us to Kobe and m heart is that in writing this book I am leading you to the Holy Spirit. When we read the second chapter of Acts we see the presence of the Holy Spirit changes things. It wasn't just a thing that they talked about experiencing but the power was tangibly evident. It says there were many wonders that happened in their midst. Their gatherings were powerful! I asked a few people a number of months ago how a Christian event they attended went. Powerful is the word they chose to use to describe their conference experience. When I asked why it was powerful, they spoke of the speakers being so good, the band being unbelievably gifted, and they also got to meet their spiritual heroes. Wow, I thought to myself, that does sound like a great event but I wouldn't describe it as *powerful*. If I want a good band coupled with good speakers, oh and not forgetting meeting my heroes, I don't have to go to a Christian event to find that. I can find all those elements at a Tony Robbins total immersion event! We have mistaken the power of the Holy Spirit for the power of well-put-together events. Spiritual power is something that will leave you completely changed when you encounter it—positive or negative. The one thing I know is you can't stay the same.

The early church was filled with power and many wonders in the midst of their gatherings. Now, I am not a f-God-doesn't-make-someone-walk-out-of-a-wheelchair-in-service-then-it-means-it-wasn't-powerful kinda guy, but hear me out for a second. Those things were happening in Acts and there are signs and wonders that do follow those that believe in Christ. We ought to be expectant that a

God who is almighty can do the unthinkable when we gather while at the same time not fixating ourselves on experiencing that alone. We don't do this so that we can go "woopty doo! God did a cool trick in church today!" But rather our love for God and one another compels us to want to see the sick healed.

I personally know how big of a difference having power makes because I come from a place that has eighteen-hour power cuts at times. I remember going three days with no power at our house in Zimbabwe. It was a horrible experience, especially considering that my wife and I had just come back from the U.S. We waited and waited and the epic sound that every Zimbabwean knows all too well of the refrigerator switching on just wouldn't come. Our phones were dying and we were having to find coffee shops in different areas or places with generators to charge up. We had no internet and to be honest it was so hard to stay up later than 7:30pm because it was cold and scary. Without power there was no warmth, no security, no light, no means of communication, and community was scarce. Everyone was staying at home just in case the power came back on. The Church is the same when we lack the power of God in our midst. It becomes a cold, unsafe place to share your difficulties, and communication feels dry and scarce too. That is why the new generation is running away from faith and trying to find where to charge up in different places—because we have powerless churches. We need the evidence of God's power back in our churches so that His presence is undeniable to those who are on the outside.

The power of God has been brought down to a good band and a guy who can make you laugh or tell good stories. Is it through those things that we hope to see lives that are hooked to the enemy's vices set free? The power of sin broken? The hype of the world overcome by the hope of the gospel? A good band and humor? That is the major difference between what I read in the Bible and what we experience in our churches today. We have settled for what is in our power to control and have abandoned leaning on the power of the Holy Spirit. I believe whether we know it or not our hearts long for the power of God to sweep through our churches. This is what the people in that first church meeting in Acts experienced. But with us, on Instagram, pastors parade their celebrity friends and when their exorbitant lifestyles are brought to question they are tongue tied. But hey, they are godly because they are funny. Then we see pastors walk away from Jesus and all I can think is, did they ever actually encounter the power of God in their time in ministry? How do you walk away from powerful Holy Spirit encounters and write it off as something natural? The honest truth which may be hard to hear is that many of us have not truly encountered the power of God. We haven't seen that power manifest by witnessing people being healed or had accurate prophetic words being spoken, and we haven't experienced it by seeing the supernatural unity that the Holy Spirit brings.

Jesus in common is everything in common.

There was supernatural unity in the early church because the Bible says that they had everything in common. That sounds like a little bit of a stretch at first glance. These people didn't even speak the same first language at the beginning of Acts and now they have everything in common? See, having everything in common in today's terms didn't mean that they all rooted for the same sports team. It meant that they were now transformed and all consumed by Christ! See, when Jesus is your everything, and you have that in common, then you have everything in common. This community was a Jesus community. It wasn't cliquey and it wasn't segregated like our churches today. Now sure, when we read later on in Acts we find that discrimination and cliquey-ness creep in but by no means was this the intent of how the Church should be.

The notion of having everything in common because you have Jesus in common should make it easy for churches to hang out together and frankly should lead to us being able to worship with people who don't look like us. I have to say that it is sometimes even hard for me to be myself in the church that I work for due to the style being so different to what it was like back home. I'm a black Zimbabwean who lives in Doylestown, P.A. and some of the way we "do church" is so far from how I have experienced it in Africa. It just doesn't feel like church does in Zimbabwe—there are no dance breaks and people flooding the front to dance before the Lord. It can at times feel little rigid, but I love that it stretches me and allows me to be in community united in Christ rather than united i preference. I stay because we have Jesus in common and also because I have bills to pay! Just jokes! Church can be one heck of a cliquey place and we as Christians miss the lowest hanging fruit when we fail to step out and unite under the banner of Christ with people who look and sound different to us.

The Church, before denominations, had one doctrine and it was sound. If you wanted Jesus, this was it. There was no separation due to man-made barriers between us and Jesus makes it clear that this was His desire for the Church in His prayer in John 17.

> 21 that all of them may be one, Father, just as you are in me and I am in you. May they also be in us so that the world may believe that you have sent me.

Jesus asks that we be one so that the world may believe! Is that too much to ask for? I think a lot of how we do church is us answering Jesus by saying, "Yes, it is Jesus. Yes it is too much to ask for." We would probably say that it is too hard to be united because they... fill in the blank. Black church is too long, white church is too short, Latino church is way too confusing and Asian church is way too formal. We will find ways to separate ourselves even as God exhorts us to oneness for the sake of a world that is lost and dying.

We are taught the lie from a very early age that there is no common ground in Christ when the Bible clearly shows us that in Him is where all the common ground is found.

But we like cliquey, we don't like saying sorry, and we love being exclusive—especially when we're on top. But despite Drake telling us to trust him that the top isn't lonely so we ought to scramble to get there, Christianity is not a competitive sport. We need to stop trying to gain a competitive edge over our local competition but rather we need to be working together to find better ways of loving our community together.

Before I talk about competition in the Church I just want to bring full circle the issue of segregation and the Church. No matter what country you go to you will find there is a history of segregation that the Church endorsed even if it was just by its silence. Some burnt crosses, some didn't speak up against the slaughter of other tribes, and some just double-crossed and swindled African kings out of their property, at gunpoint, with a Bible in hand. We may not be the ones who perpetrated this but we are definitely putting an exclamation point at the end of that sentence by not seeking ways to break that history.

If I was a singer, chances are stations like K-LOVE wouldn't play me regardless of the genre, and as an author I already know that the Christian market doesn't have room for unknown books written by people who aren't white. I say that not as a pity party but rather because it must be said out loud. Our own lack of initiative to read books by non-white authors must be confronted and faced with honesty. We can no longer glaze over our apathy and pretend that everything will be okay. If you stopped reading this right now and looked at your Christian litera ture bookshelf you will see that the evidence is overwhelming. I confess, my bookshelf is the same five white men and the same five white women you have on yours too. Throw in a Michele Obama autobiography and a bald Asian dude and that's it! I don't even see the books written by unknown black people like me. Zondervan isn't trying to sell me those books, they aren't about that life! As I write this I find myself back at that rugby game wondering about the policies that are in place at those Christian companies —the kind that guarantee that a young Joshua Harris gets a shot but will only give that same shot to black pastors that have hundreds of thousands of followers. It is a question that must be asked of the Church and the things we consume. Why are speakers at conferences like Catalyst and Passion overwhelmingly Caucasian? Those places have incredible opportunity to pave a new road and yet they continue to dish out what the people want and not what the gospel commands. Unity is an issue in our world today but those driving the car are making active decisions to maintain the status quo.

Just imagine with me for a second. Imagine the power of predominantly white Christian publishers doing something to change that, even just during Black History Month; or the power of predominantly white owned radio stations doing the same. Or how about churches doing that in February? A month of black preachers at white churches and white preachers at black churches? How awesome would that be? I think it would be powerful but the reality is our committees, our ratings and our sales... they rule the day, not Jesus! So we settle for the way things are and we miss out on what is powerful. Did I just use the word "powerful" to describe a way of doing church? Yes! I believe this is not a cool band or a hilarious speaker but rather a counter-cultural force that is only possible with the power of the Holy Spirit leading us. The things I described above can't happen without the Holy Spirit being present or else they would be happening already!

CHURCH IS COMPETITIVE

I can't imagine what it would have been like to be in a community that was wholly devoted to Christ in the way the early church was. They sat and just soaked in the teachings of the apostles, had food and prayed together. I have seen the ugly side of church competition and this is on full display when pastors gather in one place. If you want to see spiritual showboating look no further than a church leaders event or just follow an emerging pastors Instagram account. It can be hilarious and saddening all at the same time. It reminds me of being a kid and playing in the sand pit with my second-grade friends. "My dad's car has electric windows" one kid would say and the floodgates of exaggerated stories would pour forth like Kariba Dam in a good rainy season. "Well, my dad's car has special wheels that can make it turbo boost like Kit!" another kid would say.

This kind of talk is the equivalent of a pastor who has growing church asking you how many people attend your church. It is a set up because they just want the opportu nity to tell you after you're done exactly how many people they have in *their* church. Then they accredit it to some smart program they started or some cool series they thought up—oh, and Jesus. Of course, Jesus was somewhere in there, but it was mainly me... Jesus and me or more like me and Jesus!

As pastors we can get wrapped up in the wrong things because as human beings we can't help but be competitive. Especially where I live now. Americans are winners man, and if you're not winning you're losing! Even when we have the right language around it we still need to have the right heart. I have travelled to many churches over the years and in almost every place I go, I never quite hear how the church is intentionally partnering with other local churches, especially when that church is growing. It is usually the smaller churches that are less competitive, that is of course until they start to grow. Then their secret mission becomes about sticking it to all the churches around them that didn't vibe with them when they were small. We remember those snubs and thus the cycle of disunity in the name of Jesus continues.

People who have been united in Christ must surely be the ones who don't have a single issue with losing for the sake of unity in Christ. There should be line items in church budgets that say, "promoting unity with other churches." Now I know many explain this away and say, well this was Jesus' word for "those guys" in "those days", but that is untrue. Jesus wants us to be one, and by far the most miraculous thing I could ever see happen in the

Church is this competitive spirit dropped and our logo's laid down for the one logo and name we all fall under—Jesus Christ!

SUPERNATURAL GENEROSITY

Then we see In Acts that they sold property and possessions to give to anyone who had need. Acts 2:45 is an incredibly powerful verse in the Bible. This is an amazing display of hearts that have been completely transformed by the gospel. I've discovered that you can find sporadic individual generosity in churches today, which is amazing, but to see people parting with stuff like property as an entire community is supernatural. Imagine if church members were selling property and possessions just so that they had a fund that was ready to meet the needs of anyone who was in their midst. I dream of a church that follows this example and has a booth set up in the lobby for people who have needs; a church that has grocery cards ready for the hungry that enter the building.

I often think of what draws people to Christ more. A large group of people with a nice place to worship and all the amenities that cater to the comforts of those who may come or a place that just has a great ability to bless those in need in their community. Francis Chan (the bald Asian dude on my bookshelf) often shares about the conviction he felt when he was leading a church in Simi Valley, California. They were in the middle of a building fund when he started to think, "Is this the best use for this money tha we're raising?" He thought of how they could do the bare minimum structurally and use the rest of this money to make an impact in the greater community. This was a church he had started in his living room that had grown to 5,000 and he was daring to follow what the Holy Spirit was saying to him. "Don't build this church into a thing that is centered around you, a place where people come to hear you speak and get fat." He was clearly seeing this when he realized that when he was not preaching a third of the church wouldn't show up.

The more I hang out in the back end of churches and conferences, the more I realize there is so much emphasis on producing a "Coke Zero-Sugar Christianity." What I mean is, we are (and I say "we" because I'm guilty of this) creating a Church that has all the great taste with none of the calories. A Church where you can consume without cost. The gospel will drive you toward a love for others that will cost you something. Some people who lead our churches spend so much time and resources trying to think of how they can get more people through the doors to experience something they produced with their hard work. In some cases pastors look more like good business people rather than people who lead by living a sacrificial life. I'm speaking to myself here. We, as pastors, must do the hard things first. We must lead this!

When the apostles were asking people to sell property and give to those in need, I'm pretty sure they led the way themselves. They weren't going, "Y'all need to sell your property," but rather, "We sold our property to do this and if you follow us this is what we do here." Imagine walking into a church that had this vibe going on everywhere you looked? Imagine being invited to an event where the people in the room were allocating funds to help the single mom pay tuition or buy meals for the guy who just lost his job? Better yet, imagine being in a church meeting where the church was buying people homes? Now I don't mean to brag but I belong to a church like this; a sacrificial church that takes care of the sick (my own testimony speaks of this) and builds orphanages half-way around the world. That is the most attractive part of being there—but we could do more! I know I can certainly do more!

The counter-cultural nature of sacrifice is the most attractive aspect of who we are as Christians! When we lose that we may as well put our glasses back on and walk up the stairs in this rom com, cause the world isn't taking an okay-looking church to the prom. These people in Acts sold their valuables to provide for the needy. Wow! Supernatural generosity is just that. Super!

CONSTANT COMMUNITY

I am going to say something that is unpopular but it is a belief I carry in my heart. I don't think the main thing the church invested in was ever meant to be this great big gathering each week. I believe that bigger gathering is attractive for a while but close community transforms forever! Now I know that most pastors would agree that smaller community is something we should focus o because almost every church I know has smaller groups that meet during the week. Where we would disagree is the amount of time, money and energy we put into a service rather than into smaller community. The reason these communities are so important is because that is where disciples are truly made. Small groups are not a side hustle to the big gathering on Sunday but in the church in Acts we see that this was the life of the church. Our investment in production and Sunday are so disproportionate in almost every church you walk into today. If you switched the amount of resources poured into this meeting and made many smaller spaces our reach, disciple-making would be drastically changed.

You may argue that the pace of life in Jerusalem was very different to the pace of life today, but these guys met every day! I have seen time and time again that love is often spelled T.I.M.E. It is simple logic that people who hang out together more develop a love for one another quicker and deeper than those who don't. The more you actually know the people you are doing life with, the more you become like one another, and the more they become family to you. They multitasked the heck out of their meetings and therefore their community was strong. They gathered around a meal, praised God and "enjoyed the favor of all the people" (Acts 2:47), and this was the way they built community.

Close community fosters an honesty that this world is desperate to see and makes Christian community irresistible to the onlooker. If a place has a culture that is authentic and our words aren't being filtered by the biggest givers, it makes this an otherworldly movement. By culture, I mean the every day lifestyle that expresses a shared mindset and conviction in a community. We lack a level of authenticity in our churches today because we just don't know each other well enough. We don't feel the urge to gather often because we don't actually really view one another as family that can be seen daily. We view the body of Christ as some sort of a secondary, lesser family—and yet the Bible draws us to a place where this family is legit family. We ought to do for one another as we would do for our biological family and therefore the more we see one another the closer we essentially become. We start to know each other's pain and heartache. Our walls start to come down and we begin to share our dreams and failures more openly. We learn how to pray, praise, give and live together.

When we only see each other for an hour a week (or less) sitting in rows, this feat becomes virtually impossible—it becomes impossible to see spiritual growth in the way we see so powerfully in the early church. We just need to genuinely and earnestly seek to reestablish what we were always meant to be: an honest, loving, clique-free community of people who are known and loved where they are at. We are desperate for this and not the Sunday candy we get offered each week. We want the good stuff that our spiritual palates long to get reacquainted with. The more we are exposed to one another on social media and such, the more we start to just copy and paste stuff we see happening i

New York or Chicago, and without batting an eye we unapologetically move toward making our community some bootleg Hillsong church in rural Nebraska or, worse still, in Harare, Zimbabwe. Hillsong are being who they are meant to be. They're one church uniquely placed by God, with their own mandate. My guess is we're not all meant to be Hillsong. What if we miss out on being the church God meant for us to be, because we were so fixated on being some other church?

KNOW WHEN TO CHANGE

If you don't know why you exist and lose focus of your purpose, you lose everything. I strongly believe the church is morphing into this thing that lives and dies by characteristics that don't necessarily resemble the intention God had for the *ekklesia* (that's "church" in the original Greek the Bible was written in, and it means the "called out ones"). We are called out from the world to be Christ's people and this can be confusing depending on where you live, because the church we read about in the Bible were the minority and were persecuted. If you read the Bible in Zimbabwe, which is eighty percent christian, or in the U.S, which is at around seventy percent, you read it from a context of being the majority with very little persecution for your beliefs. The church in the Bible grows rapidly yet it is persecuted and is the minority.

Now, even though those percentages are high in both Zim and the U.S, we all know that it is also largely a cultural Christianity. Cultural Christianity is where we believe mainly because that's what everyone does, rather than have our own faith. This is not a good gauge if we want to see the true impact the gospel is having in a place, just like the number of bottoms in seats aren't a good way to gauge if a church is healthy or not. So why do we do church? Who is it for and what should it look like? All those questions, though clear in scripture, should be sought out prayerfully, individually and contextually when it comes to functionality. I do know this though—in our cultural climate we have to innovate retroactively into who we were always meant to be or we'll die. Big, cool and bigger can't possibly be the goal anymore, at least not for everyone. We have to spark a prayerful movement of churches that look more like what we see in Acts. If we don't innovate we will suffocate.

I read a famous story about two companies that are pretty well known today. Even though one of them is gone now and the other is thriving, the story of Netflix and Blockbuster will forever be an illustration of having a failure to read the room.

Do you remember late fees and how much you hated paying them? In the year 2000, Blockbuster made $800m on late fees. It was such a big business for them at the time. It's almost as if every time you rented a videotape they were hoping with all their hearts that you would forget to bring it in on time. It was literally a way the business made money. I would like to think that their business was being built by keeping a record of wrongs, but love doesn't do that, right? Okay, okay I digress. This late fee system which was making them so much money would eventually be a catalyst for their demise. Legend has it that a man named Reed Hastings rented a video from his local Blockbuster and returned it really late. The guy working behind the counter went to tell Mr. Hastings that he owed them $40 in late fees, which absolutely gutted Reed because the tape itself was worth way less than that. This sparked something in Reed, and he went home thinking that there could be a better way to run the video rental business. The following week he mailed some compact discs from a local music store to try out a new idea he had brewing.

This idea would later come to life as what we know today as Netflix. This $40 late fee birthed an idea that would ultimately bury Blockbuster into the ground and launch a business that is now worth $8 billion. When I hear that story I can't help but think of what kind of world we would have without Netflix. No one even thinks about Blockbuster now and yet they were practically on every block in their heyday. Netflix saw a virtual block and decided to occupy the future instead.

The Church is a mix of the two business stories I have mentioned in this chapter. We ought to be like the Boudin Bakery in how we never abandon our main ingredients, but we also need to read the times and think futuristically in how we will function. At some point we have to be way more accessible and have way less hoops to jump through, like the church in Acts. Small, simple, genuine community is the future. Believe, repent and be baptized. Worship, learn, pray and eat together often is the church on the horizon. As long as we are gathered under the name that is above every name—Jesus. As long as He is at the center, it will flourish.

THE HYPE

Who is church for? This is the question that can help us shape why and where we even have our gatherings. Some would say it is a gathering of believers for believers, and if you are exploring then just hang out until you believe. Some would say it is an opportunity for those who don't believe to discover more about who God is. Then others would argue that it's both of these to some degree and it leans toward catering to the one exploring faith. I don't think the gatherings we call "church" are meant to be purely just evangelical meetings. I don't think you have to use a certain language or water down things so that they are more palatable for someone exploring. My point in this chapter is that the evidence and the beautiful part of our gatherings is found in the life, not the production. I believe churches ought to be spaces that serve the new but when we gather we should unapologetically express worship for our King Jesus freely and completely. That is the reason we are there in the first place.

I've read and heard some people say, if we can just get bigger spaces, more influential people or even just masses of people, we would... fill in the blank. There is this feeling in the church that the thing that is missing is bigness and influence. We think these things are what make a community of Christ-followers powerful and attractive, but it's not. Those things are like a Red Bull or a shot of espresso to our souls, but just like the last night at a youth retreat, they produce a momentary change that doesn't last.

Years back a church planting mentor of mine presented me with this question: "Is it better to have one church of one thousand or ten churches of one hundred?" Even though my answer was ten churches of one hundred (mainly due to the fact that I knew where he stood) I don't think I really meant it. I thought to myself, man, a church of one hundred—how could they possibly make a meaningful impact? I started thinking how I would resent being in a tiny church. I liked big! I liked the hype and the Sunday candy! I preferred the big band, the bright lights, cool brochures and endless possibilities for friendship. Then God changed my heart over time to see how attractive ten small churches would be if they were all connected relationally. Not "satellites" but rather relationally connected, autonomous, missional communities that are all about Jesus.

I absolutely think that a church of ten thousand is not as impactful as ten churches of two hundred that are relationally connected in one specific community. These churches can reach ten different places in ten unique ways. They are small enough for people to be known, loved and cared for genuinely. We could even go smaller than two hundred, but even writing a smaller number there makes me a little bit nervous! The point is, small looks different in a world that is trying to get bigger and better at every opportunity. God's plan was for His followers to make disciples (Matthew 28:19)—disciples who would in turn make other disciples that were devoted to Christ. The plan for the Church was for it to be a counter-cultural movement that was fully reliant on the Holy Spirit. I know it's usually small church pastors who seem to say this, but we have to recognize that there is something about the grandiose church that is satisfying our flesh and not our spirit.

In this book I have talked about hype! I have brought discussion around this subject in many different areas, but I believe this particular one is the one where we can't afford to buy into the hype the most. This one we can't afford to keep messing up. If people come for the hype, and hype has a shelf life, they will leave when the hype is gone.

THE HOPE IS JESUS

But Jesus is the hope. If you get one thing out of this book, that's it! We live in a place that is in desperate need of hope. When I look around and I see my timeline and my newsfeed, it's so evident. So why doesn't all of humanity run to the hope that is Christ? Why do people willingly ignore the gift we have through the cross? The people who we read about in the Bible knew this hope so deeply that they were willing to die for it. They were willing to suffer for Christ so that others would know His love.

> 24 Now I rejoice in what I am suffering for you, and I fill up in my flesh what is still lacking in regard to Christ's afflictions, for the sake of his body, which is the church. 25 I have become its servant by the commission God gave me to present to you the word of God in its fullness — 26 the mystery that has been kept hidden for ages and generations, but is now disclosed to the Lord's people. 27 To them God has chosen to make known among the Gentiles the glorious riches of this mystery, which is Christ in you, the hope of glory. 28 He is the one we proclaim, admonishing and teaching everyone with all wisdom, so that we may present everyone fully mature in Christ. 29 To this end I strenuously contend with all the energy Christ so powerfully works in me. (Colossians 1:24-29.)

Paul says he rejoiced in suffering for the sake of Christ's body, the Church, so that we would know the glorious riches of the mystery that Christ lives in us. The hope of all of this is that we realize that Jesus lives in us. He is alive! He is alive in *you*! This hope that the world so desperately needs is on pause in you, ready for you to push the play button. It is there, ready to be activated. Jesus died and rose again so that we would reject the hype and live for the hope.

I'll tell you one last story. Five years ago I received a life saving kidney transplant from the whitest dude I know. I was dying and I was offered a new life. I took it with open arms because I knew it was the only hope. So on August 26th they put this precious gift of a kidney in me and it worked like a charm. I was on the road back to life. The first few months were painful, learning to live with a healing wound on my abdomen and a regiment of thirty tablets a day. It was a new life that took adjusting to but was way better than sickness and death.

That November, as I was healing, I was invited to a Thanksgiving dinner at a friend's house. I quickly noticed there was a big scary dog on the loose and I couldn't take my eyes off it. The owner of the dog looked at me and politely said, "Hey, I'm really sorry but my dog is racist." I was like, what? He said it so calmly and then proceeded to do nothing to reassure me of my safety. I tried to play it cool, of course, but man, it was a big dog.

He then told me that whenever people of color came by the house his dog would go crazy and try and attack them. So now I'm obviously panicking. I mean, my wife is cool and my daughter is half cool with this dog on the loose, but I'm dead. I'm blackity black! So anyway, not wanting to cause a scene I stay chilled thinking to myself a long as the dog doesn't come close to me I'll be okay. What happened next may be mainly a figment of my imagination but this dog was staring me down. I mean it looked as though it was saying with its eyes, "I'm having some chocolate today!" The dog started making its way toward me and I began to sweat. This is it, I thought, I survived kidne failure to be taken out by a dog on Thanksgiving Day with sweet potato casserole in hand. What a crazy way to end it all. As the dog got closer and closer, both my feet were up on the couch. Then events took a sudden turn that I never would have expected... the dog bit the owner! Just kidding. This dog didn't bite anyone but rather it started licking me and wagging its tail.

"It likes you!" the man said with a pleasantly shocked expression on his face.

"Oh wow! He does!" I replied.

Then the thought entered my mind... maybe, just maybe the racist dog is being thrown off by the white kidney I have inside of me!

The reason I tell you this story is because there is something in you, in us, and this something has the power to throw off everything that is dark in this world. This thing inside of you is what the passage above calls Christ in us, and it is the hope of glory! Jesus is in us and as long as we keep that in mind there is absolutely no amount of hype that can ever throw us off our hope in Him.

Jesus was all hope and He rejected the hype! Let's do the same!

I'm out.

ACKNOWLEDGMENTS

First and foremost I want to praise my savior, master, Lord and lover of my soul Jesus. This is for you and because of you. We both know how this happened and so thank you.

To the people who will actually read this... my beautiful wife Lisa, for lovingly listening to the themes, the raw material, the wack jokes and the bratty entitled version of me that flares up when I'm faced with my own limitations. For the sticky notes on the bathroom mirror reminding me who's I am. Thank you! You are more than I ever could've imagined! I love you.

My beautiful girls Hope and Nakai. I love you like 20 hundred million universes! You are both so incredibly beautiful inside and out. I am most proud of you my girls. I m happiest when I am with you guys! Find this and read this every time it doesn't feel like it.

To my Hope Over Hype crew: Ryan Peter thanks for making these words make sense bro, hope to see you here soon! Carter Bowman, thank you for helping me make this come to life dude. Dan Hagemann, for your design skills and your friendship. I am so thankful for you man. Sean Costik thank you for all your help bro!

Katie Baab, thank you for sharing your photography skills with me and for making Hershey's look like Godiva! Haha!

My precious first readers/editors Beth and Priscilla thank you! I will never start a sentence with "see" again! Zane, thanks for reading my words and not being afraid to say well that sucks! haha!

Mom and Dad thank you for doing your best. For allowing me to share parts of your journey in this book. I love you! Teej, thanks for your constant belief in me bro it fuels me to dare to believe I can make a difference. Your broken arm story is a gift! Haha!

To my pastor, Bob Myers for giving me an opportunity to grown in what Christ has called me to. Angela and Marvin Johnson, Peach and Danielle, Patrick and Danielle you guys are awesome.

The countless friends and family that have brought this book to life through your encouragement and support Thank you guys.

My Covenant Church co-laborers and church family love you guys. The young adult's crew. Thank you for letting me lead you. This book is also for you! The Summerall's and the Ventresca's for being just like family to us and letting me process parts of this in your homes.

My other pastor, Evan Mawarire. You are a gift to the

nation of Zimbabwe. You are a huge reason for this book coming to pass and your faithfulness has allowed God to use you to mold world changers. Thank you for always standing up for the weak. For always pointing us to courage in Christ and for boldly proclaiming truth even in the face of death itself. You are an embodiment of the hope guy in a hype world. Zim will rise again because it belongs to Jesus.

NOTES

Chapter 2.

See https://conquerseries.com/15-mind-blowing-statistics-about-pornography-and-the-church/, retrieved October 18, 2019.

Chapter 5.

Belleville News Report - "How much would you get if all the world's wealth and food were redistributed equally?" See https://www.bnd.com/living/liv-columns-blogs/answer-man/article170650812.html, accessed October 2019.

HuffPost, "Wall Street Got $26.7 Billion In Bonuses Last Year. That's Enough To Feed Every Hungry American" by Andy McDonald. Published April 4, 2014. See https://www.huffpost.com/entry/wall-street-bonus-alternatives_n_5000118. Accessed October, 2019.

Chapter 7.

Center for Faith, Sexuality and Gender, 15 reasons for affirming same sex relations and 15 responses, pg 15. Available at https://www.centerforfaith.com/resources, accessed October 2019.

Made in the USA
Lexington, KY
08 December 2019